A HISTORY OF LINCOLN RACECOURSE

Foreword

I have lived in Lincolnshire for nearly 30 years and have long been fascinated by the history of the County. Over the years I have contributed occasional articles to local publications. In 1997 I wrote an article of around 1500 words for Lincolnshire Life Magazine, on the subject of Lincoln Racecourse.

A few years later, having some time on my hands, I decided to try and expand my article into a rather longer work. I managed to complete the work in draft but as ever, the requirements of daily life got in the way, and I put the project to one side. I finally decided to make the time in 2020, to complete my little work and make it available, in the hope that others might find interest in the history of what was, prior to its sad demise, one of the nation's oldest tracks.

I hope that you will enjoy what you read.

Introduction

Today the United Kingdom has 60 race courses ranging from the top tracks such as Ascot, Doncaster and York, to charming country courses such as Ludlow and Exeter. Over the course of the centuries however, there have been literally hundreds of courses that have disappeared. Some were little more than fields used for the occasional hunt meeting, right up to large courses such as Manchester or Birmingham, now lost under the Gravelly Hill Interchange, or as it is better known Spaghetti Junction.

Whilst Lincoln Racecourse was never ranked in the highest echelons of British Racecourses, it could fairly be said to be one of biggest losses of post-war years, both in terms of its standing and its over three hundred years of racing history.

Throughout its existence, aside from a period in the 19th Century when jump racing was held in parallel, Lincoln only ever hosted flat racing. Business was normally spread over three meetings in the Spring, Summer and Autumn totalling seven days.

The history of racing in Lincoln is inextricably linked to its feature event the Lincolnshire Handicap or, as it later came to be known the Lincoln Handicap. It is this race, that forms the principal structure for this book.

As an aside to any readers not particularly familiar with British Horse racing the main Flat Racing season on turf starts at the end of March, before concluding at the start of March. With the advent of all-weather tracks, flat racing also takes place in the winter, alongside National Hunt (jump racing) on the turf.

I have included reference to the Classic Races, these races are the pinnacle for thoroughbred's and comprise of the 1000 Guineas, 2000 Guineas, Derby, Oaks and St Leger.

I have also diverted on occasion to make reference to some of the picaresque characters who have adorned the history of British Horse Racing.

Contents

Chapter One - Beginnings

The earliest reference that can be found to racing in Lincoln dates from 1597, making it one of the oldest known venues in the country. The Corporation of Lincoln's papers record that *'the Mayor's charges for a scaffold at the horse racing be allowed'*. A scaffold being an early and very temporary form of grandstand, generally there to enable the gentry to see over the masses! Twenty years later, on 3rd April 1617, King James I attended a meeting run on Waddington Heath, which now lies beneath RAF Waddington. The Corporation's Register recorded that: -

'there was a great horse race on the heath for a cup, where His Majesty was present and stood upon a scaffold the City had caused to be set up and which caused the racecourse of a quarter of a mile to be railed and corded with ropes and stoops, whereby the people were kept and horses which ran were seen far'.

The meeting lasted for two days and the Register further notes that: -

'On Friday there was great hunting and a race by three Irishmen and an Englishman, all of which His Majesty did behold. The Englishman won the race'.

It was James I who did so much to promote horse racing and breeding in England, particularly in Newmarket, where he had a Royal Palace built between 1605-10. The palace fell into disrepair but was later replaced by one built by Charles II, now home to the National Horse Racing Museum.

Racing seems to have taken place throughout the 17th Century across the Heath, albeit on a somewhat ad hoc basis. The Registers of the Acts of the Lincoln Corporation make various references to racing. For instance, in 1635, it was recorded that the Mayor and Aldermen had given *'liberty to deal with those gentlemen that desire allowance for a cup'*. The records further show that efforts were being made to make the races a permanent annual affair. The Corporation papers of 24th July 1669 recorded the following resolution: -

'Whereas divers persons of honour and quality out of their kindness and respects to this city and for the benefit and advantage of the citizens and inhabitants thereof, have a desire that one or more horse-races may be set up annually for ever upon the heath in the parishes of Harmston and Colby, under such articles as shall be thought fit by the trustees, viz. Lady Dorothy Stanhope, the Earl of Lindsey, Henry Earl of Ogle, John Earl of Exeter, George Visc. Castleton, Bennett Lord Sherrard, John Lord Roos, Sir John Monson, the elder, bart., and Sir Robert Carr, bart., and that lands may be purchased and settled on them and their heirs; and that in case a constant rent of 24l. per an. or more be raised, that then one third part may be employed for a lesser plate to be run for by hunting horses, and the other two parts be for the providing a greater plate, not to be run for the same day, and that no horse above six years old be admitted to run for either; and they are desirous to know what money will be given by this city; it is agreed that 20l. be for this end advanced'

Records indicate that racing had become an annual event by 1680.

By 1715 the races had their own code of conduct, the fifth clause showing them to have been very fair in nature!

If anye of the matched horses or their riders chance to fall in anye of the foure heats the rest of the riders shall staye in their places where they were at the tyme of the fall until the fallen have his foot in the stirrope again'

The first calendar recording all racing in England was published in 1727 by John Cheny of Arundel as, *'The Historical list of all the Horse Matches run, and all plates and prizes run for in England and Wales'* The calendar recorded racing at Lincoln Heath on 4th September that year, with a programme comprising both flat racing and steeple chasing.

John Cheny was later succeeded by James Wetherby who published his first calendar in 1773 and to this day, his family firm Wetherby's, provides a similar as well as many other services to the British Horse Racing Authority.

The course at Waddington Heath was a long round circuit measuring some four miles in all and included part of Harmston Parish as well as Waddington. One of the most unusual races to take place on the Heath were recorded as follows: -

'They write from Lincoln that on Thursday, seven night, there was a very extraordinary horse-race on the course of that City, between a six-years-old horse belonging to Southcote Parker, of Bilber, in that county, esquire, and one aged twenty-one years, belonging to Gilbert Colecut, of Lincoln, esquire. They ran fourteen miles round the said course, and performed it in thirty-nine minutes for one hundred guineas, which was won by the former by only a horse length. There were great wagers laid, an the greatest concourse of people ever seen there on such an occasion'

Despite the Common at Harmston having been enclosed in 1759, racing continued on Waddington Heath until it too was enclosed in 1770. At the last meeting to be held there Eclipse, the wonder horse of the late 18th Century, appeared and won a cup. Named after the great solar eclipse of 1764, the year of his birth, Eclipse was never beaten and became one of the most influential stallions in the history of racing, siring an estimated 344 winners of more than £158,000. It has been calculated that something in the region of 95% of today's racehorses derive lineage from Eclipse!

Eclipse belonged to Dennis O'Kelly (1728-87), one of the most remarkable gamblers in the history of British racing. O'Kelly came to England as a penniless young man, initially working as a sedan chairman. Seemingly blessed with great charm, he styled himself Count O'Kelly and achieved much success with ladies of society. Unfortunately, however his gambling debts caught up with him and he was sent to Fleet Jail for debtors. Whilst in jail, O'Kelly had the good fortune to meet Charlotte Hayes (1725-1813). Politely described in some historical books as a courtesan, Hayes was one of London's most successful madams. Following a general amnesty by King George III for debtors in jail, the two went onto form an unholy, if highly effective alliance, Charlotte returning to brothel keeping and O'Kelly to confidence trickery and gambling.

Within eight years it was estimated that they had built up a then considerable fortune of £40,000 and a property portfolio including a town house in Piccadilly, a stud in Epsom and the fabulous Cannon's Park to the north of London, formerly home of the Duke of Chandos.

In later years O'Kelly carried the title of Lieutenant-Colonel, albeit this was purchased from the Middlesex Militia, as opposed to be earned through any form of heroic soldiering!

Chapter Two - New Start at The Carholme

Lincoln races began again in 1773 at what was to become its permanent home, when a course was marked out on the cities West Common, known as the Carholme. The Course was laid out with the consent of the Corporation, who managed to persuade the local aristocracy and gentry to pay. In those early days the races took place in the second week of September, after harvesting had taken place. The meeting lasted for five days, later reduced to three – the Friday, Saturday and Sunday following the St Leger Meeting at Doncaster.

The course was initially laid out as an ovoid extending across both sides of the road from Lincoln to Saxilby. It is not clear as to exactly how long it remained in this layout but by the start of the 19th century, this has been replaced by a new course effectively in two parts. A nearly straight mile running along the line of the road and a circular section.

To begin with the races were a low-key affair, the poor prize money attracting only locally trained horses. The situation changed however in 1806, when a race was instituted on the last day of the meeting, worth the princely sum of 105 guineas. The cost of the trophy was paid for by the twenty-one entrants each subscribing five guineas.

In common with most racecourses of the time, the facilities on the Carholme were both rudimentary and of a temporary nature, with tents sufficing for the jockey changing areas and weighing room.

How well Lincoln had become established as a racing venue was confirmed in 1826, when the County Stand was erected, at a cost of £7000. One of the first of its kind in Britain to provide a proper viewing point, the upper balcony of the stand was often packed with parties from the local land-owning gentry, each in their own railed enclosure.

In the nineteenth century, it was common for race meetings to be run in tandem with fair grounds. Perhaps because of the proximity of the cathedral, Lincoln Races lacked this fair-ground atmosphere.

A journalist, writing in the Lincoln & Lincolnshire Cabinet and General Intelligencer in 1827, stated his disappointment at the lack of any '*phantesmegania*' or exhibition of wild beasts. He further commented that: -

'whether or not there be some regulation for the purpose I cannot determine but Lincoln race-ground presents a different appearance from most others. Even the friend of infancy, the laughter creating Punch finds no place on the Carholme. True to the custom of the city, the Lincolnian turns off (drinks) his pot and quaffs his pipe till the horses are ready for starting without seeking any other gratification'.

The Intelligencer also provides a fascinating description of the general environs of the course at the time:-

'In line with the grandstand is a long range of booths, all distinguished by some emblem, generally an election flag and all filled with company'. There are also spirit and gingerbread merchants, prickers in the garter (now known as 'Find the Lady') and civil-wills'.

In other words, despite the lack of the fair, Lincoln Races were not short on their share of confidence tricksters as well as mountebanks, thimble-riggers and pickpockets!

Evidence supporting the ecclesiastical disapproval to Lincoln Races can be found in an anonymous rhyme published at the time: -

'Ye Gulls who bet at Lincoln Races

Ye Legs who study to beguile'em

To the Castle turn your faces

Turn to yon Minster's solemn towers

Ye Vain, who wastes Life's fleeting hours'

Despite the ecclesiastical opposition, nothing appears to have dampened interest in the races and in 1830, a further stand was erected, paid for by public subscription. In addition, the quality of the races was beginning to improve, with the inauguration of the King's Purse, worth 100 guineas and the City Purse worth 50 guineas, both valuable prizes at the time.

Possibly the blackest day in the history of Lincoln Races came on 30th September 1831, when the Carholme witnessed it's one and only riot. Fighting apparently broke out between a very large gathering, of what were described as *"ne-er do wells'*, and ordinary townsfolk. At one stage, contemporary reports suggest that as many as two hundred people were involved. Many of the people involved were hurt, some seriously. In addition, tables were broken, carts over turned and the thimble pricker's booths demolished, the cost of the damage being estimated at £1000. At one point, the "ne-re do wells" appeared to be gaining the upper hand, until a band of some fifty *'gentlemen and fox-hunting farmers'* intervened and chased off the villains. What remained of the villain's carts and tents were piled together and unceremoniously burnt!

Despite the events of 1831, the races had become a major event in Lincoln's social calendar. The Lincolnshire Chronicle in July 1835 recorded that: -

'The Race Ball yesterday week, was more numerously and fashionably attended than for many years past, there being present 147 ladies and gentlemen, including the Marquis and Marchioness of Exeter and a large party of their visitors'.

The Assembly Rooms had undergone a thorough repair and were newly painted and coloured for the occasion.

The growing popularity of Lincoln Races to race goers far beyond Lincoln was illustrated by an advertisement in the Lincolnshire Chronicle of February 1836, announcing a new coach service: -

'We respectfully inform our readers of a new light horse called the Tally Ho which is to commence service between Lincoln and London on 14th March 1836. Experienced coachmen and steady horses will be employed and a rate of nine miles per hour is to be maintained. Ample time to be allowed for breakfast and dinner, the comfort of the passengers being uppermost in the mind of the proprietor'.

Opposition to the races however continued and in November 1837, the Lincolnshire Chronicle carried a report of a Council Meeting at which: -

'On the appointment of the Race Committee there was some demur at the great annual expense necessary to uphold this sport, for it was shown that, beside the interest of £6,800, the cost of the grandstand, the difference of expenditure over the receipts this year were upward of £20, making the annual charge on the town a little short of £250'.

The Chronicle had contained a report of a municipal meeting at which:-

'Mr Seely called the attention of the Council to the present states of the finances, which can be considered not in a very flourishing state, he thought it was proper time for bringing before them the annual expense changed for supporting the races. He considered that 'vice and immorality were engendered by the races and being in opposition to the consciences of a great majority of inhabitants, it was not just, nor in accordance with the principles of a reformed Corporation'. He therefore moved that no money in future be allowed from the borough fund for the upholding of the races, and in the event of that being carried, he would further move that the Race Committee be dissolved and the stand, erected at a cost of £6,000, be appointed to some other purpose, or pulled down the materials disposed of'

Mr R S Harvey seconded Mr Seeley's motion, believing supporting the races to be a very sinful practice, only benefitting the publicans, beer sellers and associated ragamuffins.

A Mr Calder, who was against the motion, thought those gentlemen who opposed the races were: -

'arrogating to themselves too much when they expected all men to bow down their heads and become saints'.

On a division there four votes in favour of Mr Seeley's motion but nine supporting Mr Foster's amendment.

Throughout its long history, the Carholme was predominantly a flat racing circuit but it did, for some years, feature jump racing. The 1846 steeplechase included two Grand National winner Vanguard (1843) and Cure-All (1845). The race was won by Cure-All with Vanguard finishing fifth.

Cure-All holds a unique place in the history of the Grand National. As well as being the only winner to have been trained in Lincolnshire, he was the only horse to have been trained, ridden and owned by the same person.

That man was William Loft, second son of John Henry Loft, sometime MP for Great Grimsby best known for his obsessive detailing of memorials and gravestones, later found to be a useful source for County historians.

Cure-All was offered for sale in 1843 for a price of £240 guineas at the Horncastle Horse Fair, at the time the largest such event in the world. The horse was found to be lame by a potentially interested purchaser and at the end of the Fair, the owner was willing to sell the horse to Loft for just 50 guineas.

Loft purchased Cure-All with the intention of riding him to hounds. The horse proved to be so good it was suggested that he be sent racing, where he soon proved his worth. That success brought him to the attention of prominent racehorse owner William Stirling-Crawfurd.

Crawfurd had entered the well fancied Rat Trap for the 1845 Grand National. Unfortunately, the horse was injured prior to the race, which allowed Crawford to nominate another horse to run in his colours. Remembering how impressed he had been by Cure-All he approached Loft who agreed, on the proviso that he be allowed to ride.

Cure-All was duly walked all the way to Aintree by his devoted groom Kitty Crisp, through wind and rain, finally arriving the night before the race looking in such a poor state, the bookmakers allowed punters to name their own price, so little did they fancy his chances.

Vanguard's jockey Tom Olliver remarked that Cure-All looked more like a Lincolnshire prize ox and would do well to complete one circuit of the race, let alone the whole race.

In what turned out to be a very attritional race Cure-All, who thrived on the wet ground underfoot, passed many a better fancied horse on the run to the line to win in a then record time, two lengths ahead of the well-backed Peter Simple. Admitting his misjudgement, Oilliver was one of the first to congratulate Loft, jokingly suggesting that Loft might have stopped off at a farmhouse on the first circuit before joining fresh for the second circuit!

Olliver (1812-74) was something a character, known for his swarthy good looks and his love of wine, women and song which often saw him, self-described' as 'hopelessly insolvent'. He even added an extra 'L' (as the symbol for the British pound) to his name, on the basis that "It is better to have an extra £ in hand'! Later in life Olliver became a racehorse trainer in Wiltshire but sadly passed away shortly before his horse George Frederick won The Derby.

As a footnote to the story, Cure-All is celebrated with his own bar at the Healing Manor Hotel near to Grimsby.

Chapter Three - Dawn of the Lincolnshire Handicap

There has been some confusion over the years as to the exact date upon which the Lincolnshire Handicap, the race for which the course was best known, commenced. Confusion arises from different races first held in 1849 and 1853 respectively. Both races have a valid claim to be the official Lincolnshire Handicap. The City Corporation produced a booklet in 1949, celebrating the centenary of the 1849 race, whereas Ruff's authoritative 'Guide to the Turf' gives 1853 as the inaugural race.

The 1849 race possessed the correct name but was held in August, rather than at the start of the flat racing season, as became the norm for the Lincolnshire Handicap, whereas the 1853 race was held in the early spring.

The first Lincolnshire Handicap was in fact due to have taken place on Thursday 5th October 1848. The race programme states that the handicap was to be the third race of the day and was to be over a distance of two miles. The rules drawn up by the Clerk of the Course, Mr John Inman, instructed entrants to pay 15 sovereigns, if declared to run. with the Racecourse Executive adding a further 60 sovereigns in prize money, which would only be awarded if horses in the ownership of three or more parties started. Since the race did not take place, it can only be assumed that there were insufficient entries.

The inaugural Lincolnshire finally took place on 10th August 1849, with 100 sovereigns in added prize money, albeit the winning owner was required to contribute E15 towards Racecourse Executive expenses.

The 1849 Spring Meeting also saw the first running of the Brocklesby Stakes, another race that like the Lincolnshire Handicap, still takes place to this day. Originally run as a twelve-furlong (one-and-a-half-mile) race for horses of all ages, in 1875 it became what it has remained to the present day, a five-furlong sprint, now run at Doncaster's opening meeting of the Flat Season.

Two-year olds are the youngest horses to be run on the Flat and given the Brocklesby is normally run in late March, it tends to be won by precocious sprinters rather than horses being aimed at the Classics, who will be introduced to racing later in the season. Having said which, the 1888 winner Donovan did go on to win the following years Derby and St Leger Classic races. Owned by the 6th Duke of Portland of Welbeck Abbey outside of Worksop, Donovan was named after a character in a book the Duke happened to be reading when he was foaled!

Despite the significant increase in prize money, the 1849 Lincolnshire Handicap still attracted only three runners. The winner, of what was an exciting race, was Lord Exeter's three-year-old filly Midea, by a head from Mr Arrowsmith's five-year-old grey mare. Midea's winning jockey Barker must have been positively microscopic, given that the horse was only set to carry 4st 11lbs!

As an illustration of how hard racehorses were worked then, Midea won the Her Majesty's Plate, also over two miles, later that day carrying 8st 2 lbs, as well as having won her heat over the same distance.

The next two Lincolnshire Handicaps went well to fancied horses a trend that would come to an end as the race began to attract more runners. 1852 showed that the race had still not become established when 'The Little Mare' walked over, something which only occurs when there is a single declared runner.

Although the Racecourse Committee was clearly trying to improve the quality of the racing at the Carholme, administrative detail seems not to have been their strong point. Inefficient management led to the February 1852 meeting turning into something of a farce, bringing with it much adverse comment in the press.

The opening race was due off at 1.30pm but by 2pm, the horse's numbers had not been announced to the waiting public nor had the jockeys been weighed out. Apparently, the jockey's weighing room was filed with unauthorised persons, seemingly interested only in delaying the 'off', most likely for nefarious purposes!

To their credit, the Race Committee moved to improve the administration of the course and, with the exception of the Judge, all the other race officials were removed for the following year.

1853 saw the introduction at the Spring Meeting of the Lincoln Spring Handicap, run over one and a half miles. The winner of the race was Cauriere, carrying a weight of 6st 13lbs at odds of 5/2 from a field of nine runners.

The 1854 Spring Handicap was won by Gregory at 5/1 trained by Thomas Dawson (1809-90) from Middleham in Yorkshire. A friendly man with a penchant for snuff, Dawson was known to his Yorkshire rivals as "King o't Moor' and by his southern rivals as 'Dangerous Dawson'. After winning the 1856 Derby with the colt Ellington, Dawson inadvertently left £25,000 of winnings on the luggage rack in an old hat box, whilst changing trains at Northallerton. Quite remarkably he had the box returned intact, after advertising for the return of a box, whose contents contained 'nothing of interest to anyone except the owner'!

Gregory was ridden by the highly successful jockey Thomas Aldcroft who was retained by the wildly eccentric Earl of Glasgow (1792-1869), a man whose behaviour could be described as both odd and challenging, even in an era known for eccentric horse race loving aristocrats.

Despite his great love of the sport and large number of horses in training, the Earl was remarkably unsuccessful, not helped by his insistence on persisting with bloodlines of proven uselessness. The Earl also had a marked reluctance to give his horses names, leading to such monikers as 'He is not worth a name'!

Apparently, in part due to his suffering from neuralgia, he had a violent temper and little or no patience with horses he considered not up to scratch. On one occasion ordering that six of them be shot, after uninspiring showings on the morning training gallops. A lover of hunting, if the foxes were proving difficult to flush out, he was as likely to choose one of his own huntsmen as the quarry and proceed to chase them for several miles across the country!

Set against, this he did take a philosophical view on his lack of success at racing, remarking that 'no one is unlucky who has an income of £150,000 a year' (around £20 million now). He also fed at his own expense a large proportion of the population of Paisley during a period of severe economic hardship and on his death, left a large legacy to one Colonel Forrester, a man he had black balled for membership of the Jockey Club with monotonous regularity!

The Lincolnshire Handicap, in whatever guise, has throughout its history generally been won by handicap standard horses, rather than those with the credentials to win a Classic. One exception was Saucebox, the even money winner of the 1855 Spring Handicap, who went on to win the St Leger at Doncaster later that year. Saucebox was both owned and trained by Thomas Parr. Originally an itinerant tea pedlar working across the West of England, Parr started training on incredibly limited resources, often having to resort to hiding in the hayloft whilst his Head Lad and jockey George Hall sought to fend off his creditors. He trained another of his horses Kingfisher to win no less than 70 out of 121 career races including the Ascot Gold Cup on two occasions.

The Lincolnshire Handicap and the Spring Handicap continued to be run in parallel until 1857, when the summer meeting was abandoned, before being reinstated in the late 1860's. The two races were effectively merged into one from 1858. The distance of the race remained at one and a half until 1865 when it was reduced to one mile, the distance it has remained ever since.

The 1858 Handicap was won by Vandermullin ridden by Thomas French, the man upon whom the young Fred Archer (generally regarded as the greatest of the Victorian jockeys) modelled his style. Unfortunately, like Archer, French was far taller than the average flat race jockey and the continual wasting required led to serious illness and his early death at the age of 29,

In 1860, Vigo was ridden to victory by 14-time Champion Jockey George Fordham (1837-77) who had won the Spring Handicap back in 1855. Unlike Archer or French, Fordham suffered no weight problems having gone to scale at just 3 st 10lbs when winning the important Cambridgeshire Handicap in 1852! He was the only jockey whole style Fred Archer could never fathom, particularly his habit of clucking like a chicken as he rode!

Despite his many victories Fordham was more than partial to the odd drink. Prior to riding Digby Grand in the City & Suburban Handicap at Epsom in 1872, the horse's owner had sent a retainer, Henry Walcott, into the Parade Ring with a bottle of port, the aim being to pep up his nervous horse. Fordham however felt the port to be too good for the horse and with Walcott's help, rapidly finished off the bottle before going on to steer Digby Grand to victory!

From 1862 to 1864, the Lincolnshire was won by aristocratic owners. Firstly, the English naturalised Hungarian Prince Gustav Batthany, whose sable lads were all required to wear dark blue liveries with tall hats and the horses clothed in scarlet. In 1863, it was the turn of Lord Westmoreland and in 1864, Count Frederick de Lagrange's Benjamin became the first French trained winner of the race.

In 1871, for the only time, the Lincolnshire Handicap was run on the same day as the Grand National. It was also the only time in which the race had ended as a dead heat, albeit the judging of such events was a little rudimentary, being down to the Chief Stewards' eyesight. The 'winning' horses were the French trained filly Veranda and the veteran English handicapper Vulcan, who was carrying a stone more than his rival. Veranda's owner declined to allow his filly to take part in a run-off, leaving Vulcan as the winner, one of twelve victories from sixteen races entered that season.

n 1872 the race was won by 100/6 shot Guy Dayrell, ridden by Charles Maidment, Champion Jockey in 1870 & 1871, and the only man to have won the Lincolnshire on four occasions, having also been successful in 1868, 1870 and again in 1873.

Guy Dayrell was owned by Henry, later 1st Viscount Chaplin (1840-1923) one of Lincolnshire's most renowned racehorse owners and squire of the magnificent Blankney Estate, which he had inherited aged nineteen on the death of his uncle Charles Chaplin.

As a young man, Chaplin was involved in one of the most notorious scandals of 19th Century society, albeit he was the innocent victim. In 1864 Chaplin became engaged to the beautiful Lady Florence Paget. Just prior to the wedding however, Lady Florence eloped with and married Henry Rawdon-Hastings, the 4th and last Marquis of Hastings.

In a century notable for wild aristocrats, the Marquis was perhaps the wildest. Inheriting a fortune of several million pounds, he proceeded to spend it at an eye-watering rate on gambling and alcohol.

Meanwhile Chaplin, devastated by the loss of his bride to be, substantially increased his involvement with the Turf and it was said by a contemporary that *'he bought horses as if he was drunk and betted as if was mad'*!

In 1867 Chapin and Hastings came into conflict again over that years Derby. Chaplin had backed his runner Hermit to win £120,000 but after breaking a blood vessel, Hermit's chances were written off and his price drifted to 66/1. Hastings, convinced that Hermit could not possibly win, backed heavily against him. Hermit did in fact go to post and was, following no less than eight false starts, brought with a long late run, to win by a head. As a result of this shock victory, Hastings lost £120,000, including £20,000 to Chaplin, who very magnanimously agreed to waive payment until his creditor was in a position to pay. It was sadly downhill all the way thereafter for the Marquis, who died aged just 26 in1868.

Chaplin meanwhile progressed to become a Tory MP and later Minister for Agriculture. A series of poor harvests and a severe agricultural depression (allied to his earlier gambling debts) forced Chaplin to sell the Blankney Estate. He remained however, a popular figure in the County and continued to hunt into old age, despite weighing twenty-stone!

Instrumental in the downfall of the Marquis of Hastings was the notorious money lender Henry Padwick. Another Lincolnshire racing figure to have his problems with Padwick was the highly popular Sir John Astley (1828-94), better known to one and all as 'The Mate'. A career soldier who, after leaving the army, devoted himself to the Turf and owned a large string of horses. Sadly he he was forced to sell his horses in 1883, after some serious gambling losses, all of which left him in his own words *'cruel hard up'!*

Despite all the set-backs, The Mate was renowned for his good humour, loyalty and generosity towards the poorly paid stable lads, a rarity in those days. In 1858 he married Eleanor Corbett, heir to the Elsham Hall Estate near to Brigg. This latter led to Astley succeeding his father-in-law Thomas Corbett as MP for North Lincolnshire from 1874-1880. By his own admission Astley was very surprised by this turn of events *'I now become a legislator! Was there ever such a parody on that exalted title'.* On being asking his opinion of Sir Walter Lawson's parliamentary Billl to ban alcohol he commented *'To tell the truth I don't know much about Sir Walter Lawson's Liquor Bill, but I do know that mine was a damned sight too high this year!'*

Later in life Astley produced a wonderfully enjoyable autobiography called 'Fifty Years of My Life'. It was in this book that the phrase *'like a duck to water'* first appeared, a reference to Sir John's shooting abilities. For good measure Sir John Astley includes Samantha Cameron amongst his descendants!

Chapter Four - Upturn in Fortunes for the Lincolnshire Handicap

Despite having been won by some good horses, the Lincolnshire Handicap was not attracting many runners and looked, by the early 1870's, as if it might be discontinued. This prospect did not however appeal to the bookmakers who, for their own financial reasons were very keen on the race. With the Lincolnshire Handicap being the curtain opener to the Flat season and the horses not having run since the previous October, there was a complete absence of recent form upon which the punters could rely, so increasing the possibility of an outsider winning, thus increasing the bookmaker's profits!

As a consequence, the bookmakers pooled their resources to increase the race's prize fund in 1874 to a very attractive £1000 in added money (prize money over and above the entrants stake money). The bookmakers and the Racecourse Committee were well rewarded by a field of 35 runners, a major improvement on previous years. The race itself was won in good style by 14/1 shot Tomahawk, ridden by a seventeen-year-old Fred Archer, his only victory in the race.

At 5'10" and a natural weight of around eleven stone, Archer was in truth far too heavy to be a flat race jockey. He existed on next to no food aside from the odd Sardine, half an orange and a sherry glass of 'Archers Mixture', a purgative devised by his doctor.

Despite being only 29 when he died in 1886, he had been Champion Jockey for 13 consecutive seasons. Sadly however, the effects of the constant wasting and the early death of his devoted wife Nellie led to his taking his own life at his home in Newmarket. He left £66K, approximately £7.3m today to his only daughter, his estimated worth having at one time been four times that but for money lost on gambling.

1874 also saw a further breakout of Ecclesiastical disapproval of racing from the Cathedral. Not aimed this time at the Carholme but directed instead at the little-known Reverend John King, vicar of the small Lincolnshire village of Ashby de la Launde.

The Reverend had no personal interest in racing but along with the Ashby Estate, he inherited his father's stud farm on the instruction that he was not to sell the stud during his life time. The Reverend continued with the stud, but the horses were raced under the rather obvious nom de plume of Mr Launde!

In 1874 his horse Apology won no less than three Classic Races (the 1000 Guineas, Oaks & St Leger). The true identity of Mr Launde was brought to the attention of the then Bishop of Lincoln, Christopher Wordsworth, nephew of the celebrated poet. Wordsworth wrote to King, taking the trouble to copy in The Times, admonishing him for his involvement in horse racing and the poor light in which it apparently placed the Church. King, by now 81 and in poor health, sent a polite response admitting to being the owner but pointing out, that he had never had a bet nor in fact ever attended a race meeting! It is thought that the Bishop might have been urged on by his over-zealous Cannon ,Edward Benson, later Archbishop of Canterbury and founder of the Church of England Purity Army!

King resigned his living at the end of the year and passed away the following year, comforted by his young wife and former kitchen maid, who he had married some ten years before. Ashby Hall was later converted into the Lake Rendezvous Club, featuring acts including Bob Monkhouse and Diana Dors!

From 1874 onwards, the Lincolnshire Handicap became firmly established as the first major race of the Flat racing season. The race also became popularly linked in the betting public's mind as the first stage of the 'Spring Double', the second part being the equally unpredictable Grand National. The bet was particularly popular with bookies, since it was difficult for punters to pick the winner of one race ante-post (in advance of the day) let alone both!

The whole history of Lincoln Racecourse was something of a roller coaster, with periods of great popularity, followed by long periods of decline. It would seem that in 1877, despite the increasing prominence of the Lincolnshire Handicap, the racecourse was in serious danger of closing. Although situated on City Corporation land, the racecourse was run by a private company, an arrangement that continued until 1939.

By 1877 relations between the City Corporation and the Racecourse Committee were very poor, the gist of the fallout being the Corporation's wish to double the rent over the figure the Committee felt able to offer. The problem being compounded by the Corporation also requiring the Committee to erect a new grandstand. In response the Committee felt able to offer only £400 per annum in rent, as well as guaranteeing that they would spend approximately £4000 on the racecourse buildings throughout the period of the twenty-year lease. A new lease was eventually signed, although it would be some years before a new grandstand was erected.

The 1878 winner Kaleidoscope was good enough to have been made favourite for the 1876 2000 Guineas, one of the five traditional Classic Races, backed to win a fortune by his owner Lord Dupplin. Kaleidoscope had easily beaten the highly fancied Petrarch on a training gallop, with the result that Petrarch drifted out to odds of 20/1. Come the race and Petrarch won with ease.

Viscount Dupplin, later the 9th Earl of Kinnoull, was a prominent parliamentarian of his day, eventually rising to the position of Lord of Trade & Plantations and was described by the famous man of letters Horace Walpole as *'fond of forms and trifles'* but *'not absolutely a bad speaker'*. He was also immortalised as a character in one of Alexander Pope's epic poems.

In 1880 the Racecourse Committee was joined by one of its longest serving members, Colonel Charles Brook, who became Chairman of the Committee in 1895 and continued to hold that position until his eventual retirement in 1926. His son Mr K A Brook became Secretary in 1895 and in keeping with the family tradition of long service, retained that position until 1939.

Throughout its history the Lincolnshire Handicap suffered from a reputation for inclement weather conditions. Perhaps the worst example being 1881, when the race was won by the great colt Buchanan described by contemporary press reports as appearing from the sleet like a 'phantom'.

The 1883 winner Knights of Burghley was trained by John Dawson Jnr, whose father John Dawson Snr had won the race three times in the 1850's and 60's. With brother Thomas having been successful in 1853, the family trained five winners of the race in all.

The winning jockey in both 1883 and 1884 on 5/1 chance Tonans was Charles Wood (1856-1945) one of the most controversial jockeys of the nineteenth century. Sad to say many of that era's greatest jockeys possessed little ability when it came to managing their money. This comment could not however be applied to Wood, an extremely able businessman and owner of the Machell House stables in Newmarket, previously the property of Sir john Astley.

Wood's principal employer was Sir George Chetwynd who, ostensibly, owned the horses at Machell, in reality many of the horses belonged to Wood, in direct contravention of Jockey Club rules preventing jockeys from owning active racehorses. It was an open secret that these horses were run to suit the betting interests of Chetwynd and Wood. The scandal was eventually aired in public by the Licensed Victuallers Gazette. Wood sued for libel and won what was a hollow victory, receiving just one farthing in damages. He was later banned from racing for ten years but returned to the saddle in 1897 when he rode 122 winners, riding the first of those winners at Lincoln, where he was greeted by rapturous applause from the public!

The Lincoln Chronicle in 1884 reported further discord between the City Corporation and the Race Committee. Disquiet was expressed at a Corporation Meeting over the Race Committee enclosing more common land than permitted. Furthermore, they were charging the public 2/6d for the big jump meeting, a massive increase on the 1/- they had been charging before, so preventing it was claimed, Lincolnian's from witnessing the finish of the races on their own land.

In 1885 the highly prestigious National Hunt Chase was held at Lincoln. Founded in 1859 the chase was, at the time, one of the highlights of the Jumps season and moved from course to course until finally settling at Cheltenham in 1911. The winner of the race was Lady Tempest ridden by Willie Beasley, whose remarkable brother Harry continued riding winners on the Flat until he was aged 85! Rather surprisingly jump racing ceased on the Carholme, just a couple of years later.

The 1885 Lincolnshire Handicap witnessed one of its finest winners when the heavily backed 11-4 shot Bendigo won in a record time of 1 minute 36.8 seconds (a record which stood until the courses closed to flat racing in 1964). Bendigo went on to win the following year's Champion Stakes at Newmarket over ten furlongs, one of the Flat Season's biggest prizes.

Just two days prior to winning at Lincoln, Bendigo had finished runner-up in the two- mile two- furlong Cesarewitch Handicap at Newmarket, conceding a staggering 29lbs to the winner. Two weeks later Bendigo was dragged out again to finish runner-up in the highly competitive Cambridgeshire Handicap, also held at Newmarket, this time conceding 35lbs to the winner! In an act of mercy, Bendigo was finally allowed to retire to the joys of the stud farm, having won his greedy owners over £20,000 in prize money.

Bendigo was ridden to victory in the Lincolnshire by the jockey James Snowden (1844-89). A highly successful jockey, Snowden could have become one of the all-time greats had he spent less time drunk than sober! Even so many Northern based trainers of the time were prepared to allow him to ride their horses, somewhat the worse for wear, in preference to using inferior jockeys. On one occasion, Snowden was so drunk he arrived at Chester, only to find that he was a week late! Another time a drunken Snowden requested trainer J Dislane to remove the blinkers from the mount he was about to ride, on the basis that the jockey was blind drunk and it wouldn't help if the horse could not fully see where he was going either!

The 1887 Lincolnshire winner, 50/1 outsider Oberon was owned by the Duchess of Montrose, perhaps the most formidable lady racehorse owner of the 19th Century, her life parodied on the West End stage in the musical 'The Sporting Duchess'. Known as 'Carrie Red' she married the Duke of Montrose when only seventeen years of age. Left a widow at sixty years of age, she married William Stirling-Crawfurd, owner of the 1861 Lincolnshire winner Buchanan and, following the death of Crawfurd in 1883, married the 24-year-old Harry Milner, forty years her junior!

Tall and erect in bearing well into old age, she dyed her hair gold, could swear like a trooper and sacked both trainers and jockeys with alacrity. The only one who lasted any length of time was 'Grim Old' Alec Taylor, who simply ignored any instructions she gave him! A man of frugal tastes, commonly known as 'The Wizard of Manton' (his stables in Wiltshire) Taylor was Champion Trainer on twelve occasions and when he died in 1943, left £593,000 the best part of £28 million in today's money!

One of the racehorse owners who employed Alec Taylor was Alfred Cox (1857-1919). Sent by his family to Australia with £100 in his pocket, on the boat over he won a part share in an abandoned sheep farm. When he arrived at the farm, glinting something shinny in the dust, Cox found that he had bought into what ultimately became the famous Broken Hill Silver Mine. He subsequently returned to England to live a life devoted to leisure!

The victory of Veracity in the 1888 gave rise to a very unusual lead article in one of the national papers. The paper's racing correspondent sent a telegram to London in which he simply gave the result of the race 'Veracity, Tyrone, Lobster' this being the order of the first three across the line. The sub-editor to whom the telegram was sent had no knowledge of horse racing, he was however familiar with a speech that Prime Minster William Gladstone had just given denouncing the Irish Nationalist politician Charles Stewart Parnell. With Tyrone being an Irish name, the sub-editor assumed there must be a linkage and added to the report on Gladstone's speech, that Gladstone considered Parnell to have 'the veracity of a Tyrone Lobster'!

The 1889 running of the Handicap went to the 8-1 shot Wise Man, ridden by that year's Champion Jockey Tommy Loates, who had won the Derby nine years before as a thirteen-year-old, weighing less than five stone. The heaviest backed horse in the field however, was the five-year-old 7-1 favourite Gallinule, who finished unplaced down the field following a burst blood vessel.

Gallinule belonged to George Baird, commonly known as 'The Squire' and a man whose spending habits were comparable with the ill-fated Marquis of Hastings. Inheriting more than

£3 million aged just ten, from his majority at 21 until his premature death aged just 32, he managed to spend upwards of £2 million.

A compulsive gambler, drunkard and womaniser, Baird's most notorious affair was with Lillie Langtry (the famous Victorian actress and even better known as the Prince of Wales mistress). Their affair was apparently both torrid and unfortunately also violent. On being asked how she put up with being bruised, Lillie replied pragmatically *I detest him but every time he does it, he gives me a cheque for £5,000*! The final straw came when Lillie went to Paris for the weekend and as a result, Baird beat her black and blue. Every cloud however can have a silver lining and as restitution, Baird gave Langtry a cheque for £50,000 and a yacht called the 'White Lady', often referred to as 'The Black Eye'.

Baird paid £5,000 for Gallinule, bred in Lincolnshire by Mr C J Hill, at the dispersal sale of horses belonging to the Marquis of Ailesbury after he had been 'warned off' (expelled from all racecourses for associating with people of ill repute!). The Marquis, normally referred to as 'Billy Stomach Ache', displayed standards of behaviour matching that of the 'The Squire'. His favourite dinner time activity being to pour soup over anyone who offended him, particularly anyone showing interest in his pretty wife Dolly. On one occasion his then close friend Baird was hit by a chicken emanating from Billy's end of the table, who claimed to have only been throwing jellies! Their friendship came to an abrupt end when Dolly temporarily deserted Billy for 'The Squire'. She later returned to Billy, as a result of which Baird had her kidnapped overnight!

Despite his losses on Gallinule, the Lincoln Spring Meeting was a success for Baird as a jockey. He won the second race on the opening Monday 25th March, as well as two more races on the second and third days of the meeting. A measure of just how good a jockey Baird must have been, can be gauged by the fact that he rode 61 winners that season, far more than any other amateur jockey has on the Flat before or since.

The 1890 running of the Lincolnshire was won by 18/1 shot The Rejected, ridden by Lester Piggott's grandfather Fred Rickaby. Like the Marquess of Ailesbury, Rickaby was 'warned off' for three years in 1902, by the Jockey Club, for having 'associations with persons of bad character'.

In 1892 and 1893 the Handicap was won by the three-year olds Clarence and Wolf's Castle, the latter being the last of his age group to win the race. Although, in an attempt to keep number of entries down, it was not until 1949 that the race was restricted to four-year-old horses and older.

The well backed 1894 winner Le Nicham was owned by Baron Leopold de Rothschild, an owner so popular with the general public, that London bus drivers of the day would attach blue and yellow ribbons (his racing colours) to their whips when he had a runner in the Derby.

The 1896 winner the five-year-old Clorane carried a record nine stone four pounds to victory, a feat not matched whilst the race was run at Lincoln and not bettered at Doncaster until 1985, when the high-class colt Cataldi carried a massive 9 stone 11 pounds to victory in the mud! Clorane was the first Lincoln winner for the Wiltshire trainer Jack Robinson (1868-

1918), the most successful trainer in the history of the race (at Lincoln) with four winners. Known as a trainer who liked to have a gamble on his horses, In 1904 won a substantial sum with a 500/1 bet, that his horses Cherry Lass and Verdus, would win the following years 1000 and 2000 Guineas Classic races.

Despite not having always been a harmonious relationship, the City Corporation granted the Racecourse Committee another lease in 1896. The principal terms of the lease provided that:

1. The Race Committee would pay a minimum rent of £400 per annum.
2. The lease was to be for the Grandstand a designated area around the stands, the paddock and the finishing post.
3. All races to be conducted to Jockey Club Rules.
4. The Race Committee could charge the admission prices they considered to be appropriate.
5. The Corporation was to be reserved a room on the first floor of the grandstand.
6. Provision for the Race Committee to sublet the refreshment rooms.
7. The Race Committee was to maintain and paint the interior and exterior of the buildings.
8. The Race Committee were permitted the right to break the lease, on giving twelve months written notice, at the end of the fourth and seventh years of the team.
9. The Corporation had the right, on giving notice, to use the refreshment rooms for other public purposes.

The City Corporation clearly thought long and hard about the appropriate rent to be charged. The City Clerk was instructed to establish the level charged by Council's in other towns, where the racecourses were publicly owned, but operated by private companies.

As an indication of the popularity of the Lincoln Spring Meeting, for the 1896 running of the race, sixty-six trains arrived at the Great Northern Station, bringing some 23,000 visitors to the City.

Despite the Corporations concerns about the Races Committee, 1897 saw the erection of a new stand. This is the stand which still stands in glorious isolation on the Carholme Road beside the golf course.

1897 was also the year of Queen Victoria's Diamond Jubilee and in common with other major sporting events, the crowds were substantially up at the Spring Meeting. That year's Lincoln winner Winkfield Pride was the second victory in a row for trainer Jack Robinson and jockey Mornington Cannon, successful again in 1900 on Sir Geoffrey. Cannon was the son of the Champion Jockey Tom Cannon, who had some odd ideas when it came to naming his sons. Mornington was named after a horse Tom had won upon at Bath, on the day of his son's birth, whereas his brother Kempton was named after his father's favourite racecourse. Mornington was Champion Jockey on six occasions and by the time he died in 1962, aged 89, he had also seen his great nephew Lester Piggott take the title as well.

Prince Barcaldine's win in the 1898 Lincolnshire, completed a third win a row for Jack Robinson, making him the only man to achieve this feat as well as his position as winning most trainer.

1899 provided an unusual link for those trying to seek the winners to both legs of the Spring Double. Early in the year Tsar Nicholas II of Russia had issued his 'Manifesto for General Peace' which related to Russia's 'right' to govern over Finland without the need for the consent of local legislative bodies! The Lincolnshire Handicap that year went to a horse named General Peace, with the Grand National going to another by the name of Manifesto!

Chapter Five - Into the Twentieth Century

As the opening meeting of the Flat Season, Lincoln Racecourse occasionally found itself at the forefront of new developments in professional racing. The 1900 Spring Meeting saw the introduction to British racing of the starting gate. Prior to 1900, the horses lined up across the course and the starter would let them go at what he considered to be the most appropriate moment. Almost inevitably the horses were not in line and quite often not all pointing in the same direction. The starting gate comprised a tape stretched across the course. All the horses would line up adjacent to the tape and the starter would then raise it so that the horses would, in theory at, least start together. Whilst the gate was most certainly an improvement, it was hardly infallible and was eventually replaced by starting stalls.

Whilst not a repeat of the similar story from seventy years before, the Lincolnshire Chronicle in May 1901 carried a report that :–

'Scores of the lowest of the low visited Lincoln with the sole object of obtaining money by fair means or foul. From the vantage point of waggonettes these bands of desperados could be seen carrying on their nefarious work. Quietly and un-ostentatiously they would approach a person apparently well to do and then, with a sudden rush the victim would be surrounded and hustled as the robbery was done'.

The 1902 Lincolnshire winner St Maclow was owned by the renowned gambler Colonel Harry McCalmont. Whilst a serving army officer and much to his surprise, McCalmont inherited a £4 million fortune from his great uncle. He took little time spending a good proportion of his new fortune entertaining his friends and becoming a major race horse owner. In 1893 his best horse Isinglass won three classic races, including the Derby, amassing prize money of £57,455 a total not exceeded until 1952. Sadly, it ended all too soon and McCalmont died later in 1902 aged just forty-one.

The 1902 Lincolnshire was also graced by almost certainly the best horse to have participated in the race, the mare Sceptre, who was owned by an adventurer by the name of Robert Siever. Moving to Australia as a 22-year-old in 1882, he made his living off high stakes poker, one game leaving an opponent dead in mysterious circumstances. He returned to England in 1888 to be declared bankrupt. A helpful marriage however to the Marquess of Ailesbury's sister enabled him to continue with his racing and gambling, including a large win on 1900 Lincolnshire Handicap hero Sir Geoffrey, part of the £53,000 he won that year.

Siever purchased Sceptre as a two-year-old in 1901 and she proved to be an excellent prospect. Dissatisfied with her trainer Charles Morton, Siever took over himself for 1902. Highly unusually for a filly being aimed at the classic races, her first outing of the year was the Lincolnshire Handicap,the aim being to try and pull off a large gamble for her owner. She was however unable to concede a couple of stone in weight to the winner. She did however go on to win four out of the five classics, and only just missed out on the Derby, finishing fourth.

The 1903 Lincolnshire winner Over Norton was trained by Charles Waugh (1860-1949), also responsible for the 1905 winner Sansovino. At one time trainer for the Newmarket based

Russian nobleman Prince Soltykoff, Waugh was always easy to spot at the races, his choice in clothing right up to his retirement in 1939 being the same as had been fashionable in late Victorian times!

The 1904 Lincolnshire Handicap went to the well backed Uninsured, ridden by the Irish jockey Bernard Dillon, later to become the third husband of music hall star Marie Lloyd. Uninsured was owned by Captain Forrester a member of the secretive yet highly successful 'Druids Lodge Confederacy', who pulled off some of the most spectacular betting coups of the Edwardian era.

The Confederacy, or as they were also known on occasion 'The Hermits of Salisbury Plain', owned the forty-box Druids Lodge Stables, located in an isolated spot on the Plain to the north of Salisbury. The Stables isolation allowed the Confederacy free reign to plot great betting coups in the utmost secrecy. It was not unknown for the stable lads to be locked up the night before a big race and, in order to avoid the gossip, often did not know which horse they were being asked to ride on the gallops!

The members of the Confederacy included an unsmiling twenty-stone Old Etonian gold speculator Percy Cunliffe and Captain Wilfred Purefoy, an investor in Music Halls, collector of rare orchids and director of the Autostrop Safety Razor company, an early rival to Gillette!

Their greatest triumph was to mastermind the victory of Hacklers Pride in the 1904 running of the Cambridgeshire Handicap at Newmarket, where various priests and a dentist from Woking helped to back the horse in such a way that the bookies had no idea as to the weight of money riding on the horse. It is thought the Confederacy were able, in today's money, to take the bookmakers for something in the region of £10m!

1906 and 1907 saw the strangely named French trained horse Ob become the first of two French trained horses to win back-to-back Lincolnshire handicaps, the other being Babur in the 1950's

Runner up to Ob, by a matter of inches, was Dean Swift a hugely popular horse with the general public, attracting adulation in much the same way as Desert Orchid in more recent years. Swift improved year in year out and managed to win the Coronation Cup, one of the biggest races in the Flat Calendar when he was eight (about double the normal winning age) and was still wining big races at ten!

Swift was owned by J B Joel (1862-1940) son of the landlord of the 'King of Prussia' pub in London's East End. J B followed his uncle Barnato Joel to South Africa, where he made a fortune from the Kimberley Diamond Field. Many years later his son Jim Joel became, at 92, the oldest owner of a Grand National winner when Maori Venture, triumphed in 1987!

In 1907 the City Corporation granted a new lease to the Races Committee lasting until 1920. The lease was on the same basic terms as the previous one.

The Lincolnshire County Archive holds details of the gross receipts taken by the Committee at the all-important Spring Meeting. From 1908 until 1914 the receipts for this meeting stayed within a spread of around £4-5000. Perhaps not surprisingly the receipts for the 1915 meeting were much reduced at £3,130. The archives also record that at the time, it cost the princely sum of £10 to rent a box for the Spring Meeting. A sum that will probably pay around a third of the cost of gaining entry to Handicap Day now at Doncaster!

The 1908 winner Kaffir Chief was one of nine winners of the race to be stabled at the Newland Street West Stables of William Sharp, the largest in the city with 38 horse boxes. The shortage of boxes on the Carholme itself was a perennial problem, meaning that for big meetings, horses could be stabled as far away as Market Rasen. The 1908 winner was obviously a favourite of Sharp's, since he renamed his premises Kaffir House.

Kaffir Chief was ridden by John 'Skeets' Martin, one of a plethora of American jockeys who came to ride in England during the Edwardian period. Champion Jockey in the USA in 1898, he rode in England from 1899, until retiring to France in 1922. The American jockeys of the period were credited with fundamentally changing the way in which British and Irish jockeys rode. Traditionally British jockeys had ridden with their leathers long in order that their legs gripped around the horse's flanks. The Americans however, rode much shorter pushing with hands and heels, thus keeping the horse better balanced.

The 1911 winner Mercutio was trained by Joe Cannon (1849-1993), the younger brother of the before mentioned Mornington Cannon and to further illustrate the tight knit world, one-time private trainer to Mr George Baird in his brief but tumultuous life. Mercutio's jockey was Charles Trigg ((1882-1945) a rider so daring on tight courses such as Epsom he earned the wonderful nickname of 'Hellfire Jack'!

The Lincolnshire Handicap was held for the last time on a Tuesday in 1913. The race was dominated by the well fancied Berridon at 100/7 and Cuthbert 100/6, who drew away from the rest of the field after a furlong. Cuthbert in fact passed the post first bur was subsequently disqualified, leaving Berridon the winner.

The Lincolnshire Handicap had been run on a Tuesday for many years, with the Bathany Plate the featured event on the opening Monday and the Brocklesby Stakes the feature on the Wednesday. There was however normally a big fall in the attendance on the Wednesday, with regular racegoers making their way up to Liverpool for the Grand National on Saturday. In an effort to counter this trend, from 1914 onwards, the Lincolnshire Handicap was moved to the Wednesday. The winner on this occasion was 25/1 shot Outram, with Cuthbert again second.

1914 saw the passing of the Lincoln Corporation Act, which granted the Corporation the right to acquire, by Compulsory Purchase, various parts of the 'straight mile' not already in public ownership. The Corporation was also granted the right to close parts of the Common and to charge admission to enter any stands or enclosures in connection with horse racing.

Interestingly the Act was published by one of Lincoln's oldest businesses, J W Ruddock's, who whilst no longer operating from their long-established premises in the upper part of the High Street, are still going strong as a printer.

Racing continued at the Carholme until 1915, when the needs of the war effort required the course to be temporarily closed. The Lincolnshire Handicap was run at Lingfield Park in Surrey in 1916, before being cancelled for the rest of the War.

Chapter Six - The Inter-War Years

Racing commenced again at the Carholme in 1919. With the euphoria brought about by the end of the Great War, 1919-21 were golden years in the history of the racecourse. Attendance figures were huge, City Corporation figures showing that the Races Committee's gross receipts for the 1919-21 Spring Meetings' were £11,450; £14,978 and £13,341 respectively. By 1923, the receipts had slipped back again to £8,232 and thereafter, for most of the inter-war years, receipts for the Spring Meeting settled down within the £4,500-6,000 range.

The 1919 Lincolnshire Handicap saw victory fall to Lady Queensbury's 100/7 shot Royal Buck, trained by Robert Siever, previously mentioned as trainer of the brilliant Sceptre, runner up in 1902. Following being 'warned-off' by the Jockey Club in 1907, Siever had returned to racing in 1912 based at Fitzroy House, Newmarket.

1920 saw the start of what was to be the Races Committee's final lease of the course, for a term lasting until 1939.

The Lincolnshire Handicaps of 1920 & 1921 fell, in typical fashion, to 33/1 outsiders. The 1921 winner Soranus was ridden by the Australian Bernard 'Brownie' Carslake (1886-1941). A much-travelled man, Carslake rode his first winner in England in 1906 on the aptly named 'The Swagman'. He later became Champion Jockey in Austria, until the outbreak of war, when he escaped to Rumania and later Russia, where he was Champion Jockey in 1916. The Revolution saw him flee once again, this time to Britain, accompanied by a large sum of worthless roubles!

The 1922 Lincolnshire Handicap provided ten times Champion Jockey Steve Donoghue with his first victory in the race on 20/1 shot Granley. The horse's owner Jimmy White is believed to have won over £40,000 as a result of the horse's victory. White was one of the most fearless gamblers of the 1920's. The son of a Rochdale bricklayer, he had little in the way of formal education. Beginning work as a ten-year-old, he later moved to London and made a fortune in finance. Sadly, he was wiped out by the Stock Market crash and committed suicide at his Wilshire mansion.

Steve Donahue was successful again in 1925 on the French trained 5/1 favourite Tapin. The following year, Steve's son Pat brought home the 100/1 shot King of Club's to beat the favourite Zionist by the head. Ironically Steve Donohue was plumb last on Argeia this time round.

1926 saw the retirement, at the age of 87, of Colonel Brook as Chairman of the Races Committee, after forty-six years of service. His son Mr A K Brook had meanwhile become Secretary of the Committee.

The 1929 race witnessed victory going, for a second time, to a 100/1 outsider. On this occasion to Elton, trained by Newmarket based Harvey Leader, who came close to winning the last running of the Lincoln at the Carholme in 1964, when his highly rated filly Fairy Astronomer, was a very close second to 33/1 shot Mighty Gurkha.

By 1929, the Carholme was going through one of its periodic slumps. Both Monday and Tuesday were poorly attended and although Wednesday was better, it was hardly comparable with the boom years earlier in the decade. It should perhaps be remembered that by 1929, the country had slipped into the Great Depression.

From 1930 to 1933, the Lincolnshire Handicap kept to its usual form with outsiders taking the prize. The only exception being the 1931 winner Knight's Error, a second success for Champion Jockey Freddie Fox, at 100/9. The other winners were Jerome Fandor at 40/1; Dorigen also at 40/1 and the French horse Leondis II at 66/1. Leondis II was owned by Marcel Boussac who was the leading owner for the flat racing season in both 1950 and 1951, despite the fact that all of his horses were trained in Chantilly in France and not the United Kingdom.

1930 also saw one of the Carholme's occasional first when that year's Lincolnshire Handicap became the first major race in Britain, to feature an on-course Tote. The Tote operated out of temporary wooden ticket offices in the Silver Ring and Tattersalls stand, later replaced by permanent structures. Approved by Parliament, The Tote (or Totalisator as it was more formally known) was introduced by Parliament in the late 1920's, the prime mover being Lord Hamilton of Dalzell. The intention being to set up a rival to the bookmakers, in order to ensure that betting activity contributed to the general good of the horse racing industry. Chronically under-founded for years, it was not until the 1970's, under the chairmanship of former Labour MP Woodrow Wyatt that the Tote finally became a really effective force.

The 1933 Spring Meeting was run in atrocious weather with Lincoln flooding so badly, the open day of the meet had to be cancelled for the first time in its history.

1934 was a good year for racing in the county, the Lincolnshire Handicap was won by the Johnny Dines ridden 100/9 shot Play On, trained by James Russell on the sands of Mablethorpe Beach. Russell originated from Australia before moving to South Africa, where he trained with success, arriving in England in 1928.

Interestingly the City Corporation's records show that 1934 was the first year in which the Races Committee received payment for selling the film rights to the Lincolnshire Handicap. The payment being the magnificent sum of £25 from Pathe News.

Winner of the 1935 Lincolnshire Handicap was the well fancied 8/1 shot Flamenco, one of the very best horses to win the race, and later winner of the St James Palace Stakes, feature race of the first day of the Royal Ascot Meeting. The winner was trained by Jack (later Sir Jack) Jarvis, the first of his three successes in the race.

1936 saw the Lincolnshire Handicap remain in the County for the second time in three years. The winner was Over Coat, another success for James Russell, this time ridden by Tommy Weston, his second success in the race, having won three years before on Dorigen. Weston, Champion Jockey in 1926, was one of only three men, the others being Freddie Fox in 1930 and Harry Wragg to have won the jockey's title between 1925 and 1953, such was the dominance in this period of Sir Gordon Richards. Wragg became immortalised in Cockney Rhyming Slang! A Harry Wragg being slang for a 'fag', as referenced in a 1967 Kinks song 'Harry Rag'!

The City Corporation papers from 1936 show that in addition to the £25 from Pathe News for the film rights, the Races Committee also received the princely sum of £5-5 from Allied Newspapers for advertising and £45 from the Racecourse Betting Control Board. The following year, the BBC started paying £15-15 shillings for the right to broadcast the Lincolnshire Handicap on the radio.

1938 saw the Lincolnshire Handicap enshrined in board game history, when John Waddington's brought out Totopoly, a racing-based sister game to its highly successful Monopoly. The equine contestants in the game were the winners of the Lincolnshire Handicap between 1926 and 1937.

The 1938 winner of the Lincolnshire Handicap was Phakos. In fourth place was Squadron Castle, who went one better the following year to win for bookmaker owner Syd Oxenham at a suitably unfancied 40/1. The first and in fact shortest priced of Mr Oxenham's two winners of the race!

By 1938 the City Corporation had made it abundantly clear that when the Race Committee's lease expired at the end of 1939, it would not be renewed. In preparation, the Corporation had formed the Corporation Races Committee, under the Chairmanship of Councillor H H Leven.

The Corporation's intention was to try and arrest the long decline in the racecourse, both in terms of attendances and lack of investment. It was generally felt that Lincoln's spartan facilities were contributing to the decline in its popularity, although it must be said the windswept nature of the course and often poor weather conditions were also a factor.

The Corporations worthy ambitions were well illustrated by a 23rd March 1939 article in the Lincolnshire Echo. The article detailed the Corporation's plans, expected to cost at least £20,000, and to hopefully be completed by spring of the following year. Improvements were to include *'a new stand to hold 1500 people with fine dining rooms and press accommodation. The Silver Ring stand, known as the 'bleachers' is to be covered. The course is to be straightened so that there will only be a very slight elbow'.*

The Echo also went on to report that the Races Committee would be making determined efforts to obtain dates for three more Flat meetings, as well as a National Hunt meeting, the last jumps meeting on The Carholme having taken place over fifty years before.

The Corporation's plans were presented to the press, both local and national, at a Guildhall meeting chaired by the Mayor, Alderman W Sindell. The drawings were presented by the architect Mr T S Darbyshire, a partner in the firm of Yates, Cook & Darbyshire. The firm were leaders in the design of new stands, having carried out work at Brighton, Goodwood and Hurst Park Racecourses.

Mr Darbyshire explained that it was intended setting the course back from the road, which would help both to straighten out the track and lessen the effect of the 'elbow' that existed at the junction of the straight and round tracks, although it would not be possible to take the 'elbow' out completely. Work had in fact already started in building up low lying land around the course.

The most important improvement was to be the new stand, which was to be built on the site of the existing County and Tattersalls Stands. The building was to have something of an 'art deco' feel to it and would be similar, albeit on a smaller scale, to the new stand at Kempton Park.

The roof of the stand would be cantilevered, in order that there would be no impediments to viewing from support stanchions. Very much the norm today but quite advanced for the 1930's. The sides of the stand would be glazed, which would provide a welcome respite from the often-biting wind.

At the end of his presentation Mr Darbyshire suggested that this was only the start of further major improvements.

Councillor Leven confirmed that at this stage, his Committee had not formally approved the plans, since 'negotiations' were still on going with the current lessees of the racecourse.

Both Councillor Leven and Alderman Deer made very encouraging statements on the Corporations genuine desire to improve the racecourse, making it a credit to the City and encouraging racegoers to come to Lincoln. Councillor Leven's one major grouse was aimed at the press and what he saw, as the constant comment on poor weather conditions at the Spring Meeting. Something he felt to be rather beyond the control of the City Corporation!

The 1939 Lincolnshire Handicap, the last to be held under the auspicious of the Races Committee, witnessed the largest field to date and was won by the previously mentioned Squadron Castle, who had been fourth the previous year at 10/1.

The Lincolnshire Chronicle of 1st June 1940 contained an article confirming, that the Government had approved the City Corporation borrowing the sum of £12,400, to help fund their ambitious alterations to the course. The Corporation was legally barred from deriving any profit from horse raising, meaning that any profits earned would need to be ploughed back into improving the racecourse.

Unfortunately, the onset of the War meant that the Council would have to postpone the works indefinitely. The only way works could commence was to be shown to be of pressing necessity, which up against the threat of Adolf Hitler could hardly be the case!

At the same time the Jockey Club licence required to allow Lincoln to stage racing, had only just been granted on the basis that the alterations would be undertaken. Given the onset of the War, the Jockey Club had given written confirmation that this requirement would be put on hold.

Looking back, the postponement of these works can be seen as a seminal moment in the history of the course – the one big opportunity to put the course on a proper financial footing. Apparently postponed, in reality, sadly lost forever.

The Second World War did not bring an immediate half to racing and the 1940 Spring Meeting, was the first to be run under the auspicious of the Lincoln Corporation. Due to the constraints of the War, the meeting lasted for only two instead of three days and, on this rare occasion, did not open the Flat racing season.

The 1940 Lincoln was won by Quartier Maitre ridden by Gordon Richards, his first success in the race and at 7/2, the shortest priced winner since Winkfield's Pride won at the same price in 1897. Quartier Maitre had already been running over hurdles, a very unusual preparation for the Lincoln. His trainer Ivor Anthony (1883-1959) was probably best remembered for training Brown Jack, one of the most popular Flat racehorses of the 20th Century. Known to have a penchant for cheese sandwiches (!), Brown Jack won Britain's longest flat race, the Queen Alexandra Stakes at Royal Ascot from 1929-1934 and is celebrated by a Bronze Statue in the Parade Ring. He even had a London & North Eastern A Class locomotive named after him in 1935.

Attendance for the 1940 meeting was good, in the circumstances, and the Corporation showed their positive intentions by introducing a new five-furlong sprint for three-year olds, the Yarborough Plate with £500 in added prize money.

The 1941 Lincolnshire Handicap was won by 100/7 shot Gloaming, trained by legendary 81-year Newmarket trainer the Hon George Lambton and ridden by the seventeen-year-old Dave Dick. In 1956 Dick rode ESB to victory over the Queen Mother's unfortunate Devon Loch, who inexplicably jumped in the air and crashed on his stomach, 40 yards from the winning post. He remains the only jockey to have won both legs of the Spring Double, the Lincolnshire and the Grand National.

From 1942 to 1945, a substitute Lincolnshire Handicap was run at Pontefract. A change of course appeared to make little difference to the predictability of the race, with both the 1944 and 1945 running's being won by 33/1 shots. Like Lincoln, Pontefract had a bend before the home straight but unlike Lincoln, the final three furlongs are up a steep hill!

Chapter Seven - The Post War Years

Racing resumed at the Carholme in March 1946 and was very much a repeat of the period immediately after the Great War, when the attendance's rose dramatically. The resumption of racing was greeted with glorious weather and the Lincolnshire Handicap was won by the well backed Langton Abbott at 7/1. The horse was ridden by Tommy Weston (his third victory in the race) and trained by Teddy Lambton, son of the Hon, George Lambton.

The 1946 Spring Meeting was so successful that the overall attendance was well in excess of 100,000 people, producing gate receipts of £34,926. Even after the costs of the meeting and £15,000 for Entertainment's Tax had been deducted, the Races Committee was still left with a very healthy surplus of £13,866. The newly introduced Summer Meeting attracted 16,337 paying customers producing £12,028 in receipts and a credit balance of £7,085. Likewise, the Autumn Meeting was attended by 14,682 people producing a cash balance of £7,035 from receipts of £12,028. Whilst never as popular as the Spring Meeting, the Autumn Meeting featured the eponymously named Autumn Handicap, one of the courses major races.

It seems clear that during this 'golden' period at least, the Races Committee did have the funds to spend on improving the course. The Corporation tried, in 1946, to re-let the cancelled 1940 improvement contract but this time, the works were cancelled by Ministerial Decree.

Spring 1947 saw typical weather conditions – cold and wet! The winter that year had been so bad the straight course was waterlogged, and the Lincolnshire Handicap had to be run on the round course. This made the draw for the race vital, with those horses drawn wide effectively having to run further than those drawn against the inside running rail. To prevent the waterlogging happening again, a new flood bank was put in place.

Perhaps not surprisingly 1947 witnessed another 100/1 winner, Jockey's Treble, coming through to win under jockey Manny Mercer for Yorkshire trainer Billy Smallwood.

There was a controversial outcome to that year's John O' Gaunt Plate, when the winning horse Boston Boro, was found to have been doped and was disqualified. As a result, Mablethorpe trainer James Russell had his licence to train withdrawn, even though it could not be conclusively proved that he was responsible for the doping. He later unsuccessfully sued the Jockey Club for the reinstatement of his licence.

If the 1947 field of 46 runners was large, 1948's field was simply massive with no less than 58 runners going to post, a record for any British flat race. Apprentice jockey Ron Sheather, later to become a Classic Winning trainer, enjoyed the dubious distinction of being the only person ever to finish in 58th place in a British flat race!

Crowds were large again in 1948 and without petrol rationing, it was estimated that crowds would have reached the levels attained in 1946. Even so, British Rail laid on a series of special trains from London, Sheffield and Newmarket.

1948 saw a break with tradition, the Spring Meeting moving from its traditional Monday to Wednesday, to a more convenient Thursday to Saturday. The move to Saturday enabled thousands of fans to come from that mornings football fixture at Sincil Bank, between Lincoln City and Bradford City.

The 1948 Handicap typically saw victory go to an outsider, not surprising given the size of the field, the winner this time being the 33/1 shot Commissar ridden by Lester Piggott's cousin Bill Rickaby.

There was something of an international flavour to the 1948 Meeting, with five French runners in the Lincolnshire Handicap, including top weight Vagabond II, who was flown into RAF Waddington on the Thursday before the race.

A continual problem for the racecourse, particularly at the Spring Meeting, was the lack of overnight accommodation for horses and for that matter, their stable staff as well. The problem was exacerbated by the fact that the United Kingdom's road network was very limited, unlike today when horses will normally travel to the course and back on the same day.

The following year witnessed the Centenary Race, or at least the centenary of the Lincolnshire Handicap as run at the Summer Meeting in 1849. To celebrate the event, a banquet was held at the Assembly Rooms in Bailgate close to the Cathedral. Unfortunately, the Mayor, Councillor J W Lawson took a dim view of the event and was quoted in the Echo as saying *'It is no use beating around the bush. I look upon horse racing as one of the social evils of the day'*. The Mayor's attitude was criticised in a speech by Alderman C H Doughty, in front of an audience including special guest, the Jockey Club Chief Steward Bernard, Duke of Norfolk.

A good first day crowd on the Thursday saw a new City Flag unveiled to celebrate the 100th Anniversary of the Lincolnshire Handicap. Meanwhile shoppers at a city store, were able to benefit from tips provided by the legendary Prince Monolulu. The 'Prince' (1885-1965), or to give him his real name Peter McKay, was a colourful figure who arrived in Britain at the turn of the century. He claimed to be chief of the Falasha tribe in Abyssinia, now Ethiopia, but was actually the son of a horse breeder from St Croix in the then Danish West Indies! A large man given to wearing baggy trousers, ostrich feathers and sporting an umbrella he was best known for his catch phrase 'I gotta horse'!

Crowds were excellent on the Saturday, again bolstered by thousands coming from Sincil Bank, this time from a game with Fulham.

Following the shock results of the previous two years, an even bigger surprise occurred in the 1949 running of the Lincolnshire Handicap, when the 6/1 favourite Fair Judgement actually succeeded in winning! The horse was ridden by Eph Smith and trained by Jack Jarvis, who had been successful together in 1938 with Phakos.

The problem of overnight accommodation was so had for the 1950 Spring Meeting, that a third of the horses had to be stabled at Market Rasen Racecourse some nineteen miles away.

For the second year running, the race went to the favourite, this time Dramatic ridden by Gordon Richards, which was a major disappointment for the 800 or so punters, who had travelled down from Teesside to support the heavily backed runner-up Barnes Park.

One minor improvement at the course saw the introduction of electronic scales for weighing the jockeys in and out. Councillor Levin also announced his intention to stand down as Chairman of the Races Committee, to be replaced by Councillor Bell.

In 1951 the BBC had run into a spot of bother covering the Lincolnshire Handicap. The intention had been that the race should be followed, in its entirety, by a camera placed on top of a van racing along the adjacent Carholme Road. The only problem was, the van proved insufficiently fast to keep pace with the horses! For 1952, the van was only expected to keep up for the first six furlongs, with the final two furlongs covered by a camera placed atop the Main Stand.

1952 saw the Spring Meeting move back to its traditional Monday to Wednesday slot. il would be too simplistic to say that this marked the beginning of the end for Lincoln Races The course did however depend on the Spring Meeting and, despite the often-inclement weather, Saturday's were always likelier to attract a large crowd, than a Wednesday.

By 1952, the Jockey Club had concluded that greater protection needed to be given to race horses, to prevent their being 'nobbled' prior to the races' This was a particular problem at Lincoln, with the horses scattered all over the town. To this end, the Jockey Club's Security Chief – Colonel C T O'Callaghan came equipped with an eighty strong force to stop the race fixers.

The 1952 Lincolnshire Handicap returned to normal form with victory going to 33/1 shot Phariza, from a field of forty runners. Phariza was ridden by young apprentice jockey Dominic Forte, claiming a seven-pound allowance. To give them an advantage over older and more experienced riders, apprentices are allowed to ride their mount at a lower weight than would a full jockey.

Sad news came through just prior to the Spring Meeting that the former Mablethorpe trainer James Russell, had lost a leg in a train accident near to Hitchin. In addition, the flags above the stand were flying at half-mast, in acknowledgement of the death of Queen Mary, widow of King George V.

On the Saturday before the meeting the Lincolnshire Echo reported Councillor Bell as stating that further extensive drainage works, carried out prior to the start of the season, would nullify the effect of the draw, meaning that high/low drawn horses would no longer enjoy an advantage. Unfortunately, he was proved to be completely wrong!

Better than normal weather, the best since 1946, ensured a good crowd for the Lincolnshire Handicap, albeit not up to the level of that glorious spring. Attendances were also up by about 20% on the Monday and Tuesday. Victory in the big race went to the gambled on Sailing Light, providing Yorkshire trainer Gerald Armstrong with the biggest win of his career. Quoted overnight at 25/1, sheer weight of money brought his price down to 100/8 when the flag went down.

An innovation for the 1954 season was the introduction of race commentaries, broadcast through the public address system. By this time, most other courses benefited from this already, although according to the Lincolnshire Echo, the Racecourse Company had first approached the Jockey Club 25 years before with the idea!

Ever since 1946, the opening race of the meeting had been restricted to apprentice jockeys, thus ensuring that each year a junior rider would have the opportunity to lead the jockey's table, even if it was only for the half hour until the next race! The youngest jockey riding in the race was twelve-year-old Josh Gifford, who went on to become one of the country's top National Hunt jockeys and trainer of Grand National winner Aldaniti, ridden to an emotional victory by Bob Champion in 1981.

Meanwhile another young person was setting the betting market alight. Twenty-year-old Phyliss Bebb, appearing on TV's 'What's My Line' show, tipped the little fancied Desert Way for victory. As an apparent consequence, the horses price tumbled from 66/1 to 6/1, all of which made little difference since the horse still finished well down the field!

Victory in the 1954 Lincolnshire Handicap went to the 100/7 shot Nahar, trained by leading French trainer Alex Head and owned by Prince Aly Khan. Gallant runner-up was the previous year's winner Travelling Light, ridden this time by the now Sir Gordon Richards, in his final season as a jockey.

Probably one of the best-known socialites of the 1950's, Prince Aly Khan was son of the Third Aga Khan leader of the Nizarai Ismaili Muslims, a sect of Shia Islam. An officer in the French Foreign Legion and during the War a Lieutenant Colonel in the Wiltshire Yeomanry, he was awarded the French Legion of Honour in 1950. It was however, as an international man about town and racehorse owner that made him of greatest interest to the general public. He was variously the first racehorse owner, in 1959, to win over £100,000 in a season; husband of Hollywood Star Rita Hayworth and even name checked in Noel Cowards' version of the Cole Porter song 'Let's Do It, Let's Fall in Love'!

Despite the fact that the crowds continued to be reasonably good for Lincolnshire Handicap day, the fortunes of the course were not being helped by the steady deterioration of the facilities. The Races Committee clearly had the best of intentions and did spend some money on the course, it was just not enough.

Friday 18th March 1955's Lincolnshire Echo found Councillor Bell answering back to criticisms from 'Horse & Hound' columnist Audax, concerning the poor facilities offered by the course. Audax was particularly agitated by the state of the stands and the lack of a photo-finish camera, something of a rarity amongst British racecourses by then. In defence of the Races Committee, Councillor Bell was able to point out that, not before time it had to be said, racecourse stabling had been increased from 50 to 110 boxes, at a capital cost of £9,000.

Following on from Prince Aly Khan's success in the previous year's race, in 1955 it was the turn of his father the Aga Khan to win the Lincolnshire with the well backed Military Court at 8/1.

The sad decline in local interest in the racecourse was highlighted by a front-page article by Norman Frisby in the Chronicle on the day of the Lincolnshire Handicap. The article reported that the Corporation Transport Department had laid on a large fleet of buses to transport punters from the City Centre to the racecourse. Only 1300 people however availed themselves of the service, a far cry from just a few years before.

That day's Echo also contained an article from columnist Gossiper bemoaning the fact that the City and Union Jack flags on the stand roof looked tatty; the electric clock did not work; the footpath to the course was being made up sixteen years too late and during the meeting rather than beforehand.

The summer meeting on 8th June also saw a new departure for Lincoln Racecourse, with the introduction of evening racing, aiming to attract more local interest.

1956 witnessed a resumption of standard form in the Lincolnshire Handicap, with the race being won by 40/1 outsider Three Star II, third the previous year. As one stage the winner was plumb last, before coming through from behind to win, something of a feat in a large field on such a narrow track.

That years Brocklesby Stakes sprint was won by Gledhill, a fourth triumph for Yorkshire Trainer Ernie Davey, who started training in 1922 and did not retire until 1974, by which time he was 84 years of age. Despite working with limited resources, Davey enjoyed considerable success, even managing to win the highly valuable Ayr Gold Cup in 1951 with £50 purchase Fair Seller, a small sum even then.

1957 and 1958 saw Babur take back to back victories in the Lincolnshire Handicap. Clearly not fancied by the punters either year, he was returned at 25/1 on both occasions.

The winning jockey in 1957 was Edward Hide, who recalled in his autobiography 'Nothing to Hide' that other than the bends which were railed, the rest of the course was marked out by poles, something that would be unthinkable now. Hide remembered that on one occasion the runners suddenly found a young man riding a bicycle along the course towards them! Fortunately, the jockey's managed, no doubt to the young man's relief, to ride either side of him!

Babur's trainer was Bill Elsey whose father Captain Charles Elsey (successful in the 1945 substitute Lincoln) was born at Baumber in Lincolnshire. His father was Willian Elsey, a Lincolnshire farmer who trained a string of 100 horses at the turn of the century and in the 1905 Flat Season won 124 races, a record not broken until 1979 by Henry Cecil.

Veteran journalist Richard Baerlin's biography of the 1980 Champion Jockey Joe Mercer recalls an interesting story from the 1957 Lincolnshire Handicap. Prior to the race the hot ante-post (pre-race) money had been piling onto the colt Precious Heather, owned by the legendary gambler Alex Bird. Unfortunately for Bird, none of it was his money and he withdrew the horse rather than accepting a short price. Brid's attempt to keep the colt's prospects secret were foiled by a chance remark from Mercer his jockey. Prior to the season starting, Mercer had been on holiday in Monte Carlo and had gone to the casino to watch the action. Feeling sorry for a gambler down on his luck, he had informed his unlucky acquaintance that he could always recoup his losses by backing Precious Heather in the Lincoln. Unfortunately, Mercer's new friend turned out to be Chummy Gaventa, a leading British bookmaker of the day! Ironically when Precious Heather ran in the following years Lincoln, he failed to see out the one-mile trip, his owner having had a fortunate escape the previous year!

The 1958 Lincolnshire Handicap was the most valuable yet, with an impressive £3,460 to the winner. Clerk of the Course Malcolm Hancock reported that with Entertainment Tax (introduced in 1919) having finally been lifted, there had been something of a revival in attendances. Gossiper's column in the Echo, the day after the Lincolnshire Handicap, bemoaned again the deteriorating conditions at the racecourse, with builder's rubble left lying around the Sliver Ring. The article did however, optimistically but sadly incorrectly, conclude that the necessary improvements would be carried out one day.

1959 saw the introduction of live BBC TV coverage of the big race, although fears were expressed that this could affect attendances, something the poor facilities were unfortunately achieving already.

1959 and 1960 witnessed an unexpected trend with victory going on each occasion to the favourites, Marshall Pil and Mustavon, both trained by Yorkshire based Sam Hall, meaning that victory had gone north for the last four years.

One of the jockeys riding in the 1959 Lincolnshire Handicap was Peter Boothman, who hailed from the Lincolnshire village of Norton Disney, and had won the Yarborough Selling Plate on the second day of the meeting. Boothman had been Champion Apprentice the previous year but sadly, like many junior riders both before and since, his career faded after he joined the ranks of the senior jockeys and was unable to claim a weight allowance.

The Lincolnshire Echo on the Tuesday of the Spring Meeting carried a headline proclaiming the Races Committee's £30,000 plans for improvements. The funding for any improvements would have to come from race revenue. The problem with this being, the continually deteriorating facilities were attracting fewer and fewer visitors.

Interestingly Councillor Bell, the Chairman, reported that the Committee had not found racing on a Saturday profitable, the evening meetings proving to be the most successful.

The day after 1960 Lincolnshire Handicap, the Gossiper column in the Echo ominously suggested that unless the Corporation spent £45,000 immediately on improvements, the Levy Board (the statutory body that controls racecourse funding) would cut its grant. Problems were beginning to mount for the course, whatever the optimistic soundings coming from the Races Committee.

Being the opening meeting of the Flat season, Lincoln racecourse made history with another racing first. The Monday of the 1961 meeting seeing the introduction to British racing of the overnight declaration of runners, where horses had to be declared to run by 11.00am the previous day, rather than on the actual day. Failure to run a horse would lead to the trainer being fined, unless a vet's certificate could be produced. The aim was to ensure greater certainty in the betting market, stopping trainers from withdrawing horses without good reason, such as a vet certified injury.

The 1961 Lincoln was won quite comfortably by John's Court a 25/1 outsider. There was however, drama earlier in the race. As the 37 runners reached the elbow some of the apprentice riders decided to cut the corner with the result, that the horses bunched to such an extent that Small Sam and Penates, the mounts of Royal Jockey Harry Carr and Keith Temple-Nidd respectively, were lifted off the ground for 100 yards! When they did come back to the ground both horses fell leaving Nidd with bruising and Carr with a broken collarbone and ankle.

For 1962 the course was given something of a facelift, new ladies toilets were built, and the Tote Control building was demolished. 1962 also saw the introduction of official dope testing.

That year's Lincolnshire Handicap saw the outsiders again to the fore, with victory going to 50/1 shot Hill Royal, trained by the previous year's victor Eric Cousins. On this occasion the horse was ridden by Joe Sime, as opposed to Johnny Greenway who was down to ride but had to withdraw, on account of his having to put up two pounds overweight. Hill Royal's victory was more surprising have been drawn four, a traditional graveyard for a horse's chances.

Chapter Eight - The Beginning of the end for Flat Racing

Despite the cosmetic improvements that had been made, dark clouds were circling over the Carholme. An article in the Echo on 28th March 1962, following that years Spring Meeting, reported that it might be the last to be held at the Carholme. Clerk of the Course Major Malcolm Hancock however, assured the Echo that the future of the course was safe for another five years, albeit over £100,000 in capital funding would be required! Hancock further reported the Course Executive were two years through a £30,000 seven-year programme of phased improvements.

Public and media comment on the deteriorating condition of the course and facilities at the Carholme was however not going away. In answer to this, the Echo on 6th March 1963, contained an article quoting the Town Clerk as saying that, the Corporation had improved matters since taking over in 1939, having inherited buildings that we are in a deplorable state. The Town Clerk further reminded readers, it had always been a requirement of the Corporation that the racecourse should be self-supporting and not reliant on income from the rates. Apparently, the course had only made a profit seven times in the last nineteen years, giving a gross loss of £3,070, as compared with the £35,000 the Corporation had spent on maintenance and improvements.

The Corporation had by this time submitted plans to the Horse Racing Levy Board (the organisation set up in 1959 by the Government to distribute betting tax to support the countries racecourses) for £150,000 worth of improvements to the racecourse. The works proposed would include a new stand to replace the existing ones and the 'elbow' in the 'straight' mile would finally be eradicated. This was reported in a front-page article in the Echo on 16th March, quoting from Councillor Leslie H Priestly, Chairman of the Races Committee. It was also reported that, in a continuing show of optimism, the Corporation was applying for an additional day's racing to supplement the exiting seven, three in the spring, two in the summer and a further two in the autumn.

The 1963 Spring Meeting got off to a poor start, with Monday typically cold and windy, resulting in attendances being down on the previous year. Major Hancock also pointed to the televising of the meeting and the recent opening of betting shops as being factors.

The Lincolnshire Handicap saw victory and record prize money of £4,089 go to the 50/1 shot Monawin, only the third filly to win in the 20th Century. In yet another year for outsiders, the runner-up Kalomoss came in at 40/1, the third at 25/1 and the dead-heating fourth placed finishers at 66/1 and 25/1. The winner was again ridden by Joe Sime, his third victory in the race.

Monawin was both owned and trained by Ron Mason, who had a less than conventional entry into the world of professional horse racing. A one-time speedway star, racing out of Manchester's Belle Vue track, Mason was later a partner in a Dublin garage business. In 1956 he went to a race meeting with the object of selling a car to the legendary Irish jockey and trainer, Aubrey Brabazon. Surprisingly for a car dealer, Mason fell for Brabazon's legendary sales patter and rather than selling him a car, he left having purchased a racehorse named Fuel for £600! As luck would have it the horse went on to win the Irish Lincolnshire Handicap.

Whatever the laudable aims of the Council, both the local populace and racing fans in general were sadly turning their backs on the Carholme. Attendance for Handicap Day in 1960 was 11,949; for 1961 it had slipped to 11,165; 1962 it was down to 11,082 and for 1963 just 9,800. Even allowing for the coming of television, this was still a dramatic decline on the 38,530 present on Handicap Day 1946 and a far steeper decline than had been witnessed by comparable racecourses.

For some time rumours had been circulating that there would be a rationalisation in the number of racecourses operating in Britain. The problem being that many of the country's courses, not just Lincoln, had suffered chronic under investment over many years and the Levy Board's funds would only stretch so far.

It was on Friday 5th April that Field Marshall Lord Harding, the Chairman of the Levy Board, made the announcement that Lincoln would be one of twelve courses, for whom 'in the general interests of racing further support cannot be justified after 1966'.

According to Lord Harding, in an article by the highly respected Tim Fitzgeorge-Parker in the Daily Mail, approximately £15 million would be required to modernise all of the nation's courses and that level of funding just did not exist. Instead funding of £4 million would be spent, over the next three years, on what Lord Harding described as a 'Division One' of twenty courses. These courses comprised the major venues such as Ascot and Doncaster and smaller courses, such as Ludlow, which had put forward proposals for modernisation, which were believed to be realistic. The decision on which courses to support was based on a number of criteria, with priority given to issues including security of tenure, financial position, quality of racing and geographical location of the course.

Below the 'First Division' was a 'Second Division' of courses who could receive limited funds for modernisation but would not receive funding for major projects, as and until it became available.

Reasons were given to relegate the various other courses. In the case of Lincoln, it was because it 'had poor amenities which made it unpopular with all racing interests and with the public...A disproportionately large sum would be needed for the rebuilding required' a harsh verdict perhaps but sadly one containing large elements of truth. It was unfortunately also true that many jockeys were not sorry to see the course under threat - disliking the tight nature of the course, the often biting wind and once again the poor facilities.

Of the twelve 'relegated' courses, Lewes, Rothbury and Woore Hunt in Shropshire, closed shortly after the announcement. Bogside and Stockton struggled on for some years and Edinburgh, Pontefract and Sedgefield still survive, with their Levy Board funding reinstated. Folkestone also had its funding reinstated but sadly closed for good in 2012.

Relegated courses were still free to operate, as long as they were being granted fixtures by the Jockey Club. Lord Harding expressed the hope that, like their counterparts in rural France, these courses, with their inevitably lower prize money available, might prove valuable outlets for *'bad'* horses. However, the reality was that even with Levy Board funding, courses such as Lincoln, were barely viable, let alone trying to operate without that funding.

Understandably the news of Lord Harding's announcement was met with anguish in the local media. That evening's Lincolnshire Echo described the announcement of Lord Harding's news as *'a slap of face for racing in Lincoln, so soon after the announcement of a scheme requesting £150,000 of funding from the Levy Board for improvement's'*. The article went onto quote Councillor Priestly as saying *'I don't accept defeat easily on anything'*. In a long interview he went on to pledge that every effort would be made to try and keep racing going. An emergency meeting of the Races Committee would be held the following Tuesday.

Councillor Priestly said he felt disappointed that the Levy Board had not properly appreciated the improvements that the Committee had made already improvements, from its own funds, at the Carholme. He also went on to suggest that the Council would try *'private sources'* to fund flat racing and look into the possibility of bringing back National Hunt racing. Other ideas included putting a running track in front of the stands, although quite where the funding would come from for this idea was not explained. Of particular importance to Councillor Priestly, was the need for the people of Lincoln to come out and support the racecourse for the summer meeting.

The upshot of the Races Committee's emergency meeting was that a formal decision was taken to appeal against Lord Harding's decision.

Efforts to keep the flag flying at the Carholme were still being made and on 22nd October 1963, Ladbrokes announced that they had agreed to put up £3,000 in added prize money for the following years Lincolnshire Handicap. Director F R Kaye stated that *'when we heard that the Levy Board were not going to support Lincoln, we felt it imperative that the Lincolnshire Handicap should remain, and we are very pleased that the Lincoln Committee have accepted our offer'*.

On accepting Ladbrokes cheque, the new Chairman of the Races Committee Councillor S A 'Jock' Campbell stated that racing would continue indefinitely at Lincoln. A brave but perhaps somewhat bold statement, given the fact that the Levy Board had turned down Lincoln's appeal, although the ultimate decision belonged to the Home Secretary Henry Brooke.

Ladbrokes news was welcomed by Clerk of the Course Malcolm Hancock who advised the Echo that, the increase in prize money would help the race keep pace with other important handicaps and he was sure that the move *'will put new life into Lincoln racing'*.

Encouragingly the threat of closure did seem to engender support for the racecourse. In January 1964 on BBC Television's 'Look North', Councillor Campbell confirmed to interviewer Keith Macklin that Billy Butlin had pledged £1000 in sponsorship for the apprentice's race that opened the Spring Meeting. To be known, none too surprisingly, as the 'Billy Butlin Apprentices Handicap'.

When asked the question by Keith Macklin *'is racing in Lincoln safe for another year or two'*, Councillor Campbell replied *'it depends on the public. If they go along in their thousand's we shall keep racing in Lincoln for a long, long time'*. The Echo led with the headline *'they must go in their thousands to Carholme'*. The question was, would the people of Lincoln head the call?

Elsewhere that evening's Chronicle contained a lengthy article talking up prospects for the Spring Meeting, as well as an advertisement inserted by the Races Committee, urging the local populace to support the course.

The article contained a message from Billy Butlin, who would not be able to attend his race on Monday, expressing the hope that the Spring Meeting would be a major success and would lead to a change of heart on the part of the Levy Board, toward the future of racing in Lincoln.

Race entries were over 200 up on the previous year, the photo-finish camera would be in use for the first time; spectators in the stand could view the start by way of closed-circuit television (another first); a mobile telephone exchange would be on site; a large refreshment marquee erected and additional temporary stabling provided. Most importantly prize money was to be at a record level of £13,600 of which £7,600 came from the Lincoln Executive, £1,600 from the Levy Board with the remainder coming in sponsorship. The Lincolnshire Handicap was to be worth a record £4550 to the winner.

Monday 16th March 1964 dawned windy but bright. The big question being, would the Committee's and the sponsors efforts be enough? Sadly, the answer was no they were not. Only 1150 paying customers attended, bringing in receipts of just £1,307. One customer there to see his horse "You'll be so Lucky" run in the opener, was the hugely popular comedian Al Read. Unfortunately, his presence proved no more of an attraction to the public than the racing. The son of the owner of a sausage making factory in Salford, Read was best known for his catch phrase 'Right Monkey'. His radio show in the 1950's regularly attracted audiences of 35 million listeners a week!

Tuesday proved to be no better, with just 1085 customers, 900 down on 1963 and producing receipts of only £1,259.

As always Lincolnshire Handicap day produced a much healthier crowd, with a total paying attendance of 8,585 and receipts of £8,256. Even this however, was 1,215 less paying customers than in 1963. The Handicap itself went yet again to an outsider, the 33/1 shot Mighty Gurkha. The winner was ridden by Peter Robinson and trained by Teddy Lambton, successful back in 1946 with Langton Abbot.

On 27th April 1964 the Echo carried an article commending the valiant efforts being made by the Races Committee to try and retain the Jockey Club's interest in the course (as the body that allocated fixtures). The Committee's new task was to try and persuade the Jockey Club to grant the Spring Meeting a date for 1965, allowing the Lincolnshire Handicap to be run on a Saturday. The advent of the TV age had shown that only races of truly national importance, such as The Derby, could hold their own midweek, others needed a weekend date to retain their success.

The next meeting to be held on the Carholme took place on 20th & 21st May, with Councillor Campbell still vowing to fight *'tooth and nail'* to keep racing going at Lincoln. Poor weather greeted racegoers on the opening day but the attendance was up, albeit not to the level the

Committee's efforts needed. That day's Echo contained a picture showing two Leeds based bookmakers, wearing black top hats with *'RIP Lincoln must we mourn the loss of the grand old racecourse'* Councillor Campbell publicly thanked the bookies for their albeit macabre support.

The last race of the meeting and sadly as it transpired, the last flat race to be run at the Carholme, was the Cranwell Stakes, held over a straight seven furlongs. The race was won by Twinkle Dee, ridden by Royal Jockey Harry Carr and trained by Newmarket based Bruce Hobbs. As a 17-year-old, Hobbs rode Battleship to victory in the 1937 Grand National, a horse with the unique record of being the only one to win both the British and American Grand Nationals.

The Races Committee continued with its efforts to keep racing on the Carholme but the final nail in the coffin came through on the 9th June, when the Jockey Club confirmed that they would not allocate the course any more fixtures after the end of the 1965 Flat season, a year prior to when the Levy Board support had been due to expire. Councillor Campbell expressed himself to be *'bitterly disappointed'*.

Equally upset was Lincoln Labour MP Dick Taverne who had been amongst a small group of MP's campaigning to save Lincoln and the other courses under threat. Taverne's approach had been to argue that the Levy Board had no moral grounds for discriminating against any single course. At one stage he believed that he had convinced Joint Under Secretary of State Christopher Woodhouse of the justice of this view. Sadly, this was not to be the case.

Marcus Kimball the Conservative MP for Gainsborough asked the Home Secretary Henry Brooke could he *'tell me who actually makes the final decision on the allocation of fixtures'*? Brooke gave a somewhat woolly answer, ignoring the fact that the final decision to ratify the Levy Boards decision lay with him.

Inevitably news came through on 21st July 1964 that the Home Secretary had ratified the Levy Board's decision, meaning that there was now no way back for Lincoln Racecourse. All of Councillor Campbell and his Committee's considerable efforts had been in vain.

The following night's Echo carried the news that at a meeting lasting just twenty minutes, the City Council had taken the decision to abandon the race meeting planned for 16th & 17th September and to close the course with immediate effect. There was only one dissenting voice, apparently willing to carry on what would have been a hopeless fight.

The City Council stated publicly that they were *'most aggrieved at the decision'* and they considered it *'extremely unfair to deny them (the Races Committee) a share of funds from on and off course betting and they felt that they are being forced out of business in a way which they deplore'*, the statement went onto thank everyone who had fought to save the Carholme but without future fixtures, immediate closure was the only option.

The decision not to proceed with the September meeting was taken due to the fact that the Autumn Meeting usually lost money and, with no more Lincolnshire Handicap's to subsidise it, the cost of the meeting could not be justified.

Ironically Councillor Campbell had been unable to attend the final race meeting, due to having accepted a prior invitation to attend a Royal Garden Party at Buckingham Palace.

Mr J F Littleover the Chairman of the Races Committee in 1946 and one of the original Committee, which took over the course in 1939, expressed the unsurprising view to the Echo that the closure was a tragedy. He went on to exonerate the Races Committee from any blame, admitted that there had not been enough public support for the course (a mild chastisement) and blamed those within the racing industry for not properly supporting Lincoln.

It was quickly decided that the Lincolnshire Handicap would be transferred to Doncaster Racecourse, where it remains to this day, known from 1965 onwards as the Lincoln Handicap. The Tote buildings and numbers were removed to Fakenham.

Chapter Nine - New Beginnings for Racing on The Carholme

The 1964 closure of the course appeared to be that, as far as racing on the Carholme was concerned. There was however to be one last hurrah. Negotiations began late in 1965, between the City Council and the newly formed Carholme Point to Point Committee, the aim being to use the course for point-to-point racing. The Committee comprised representatives from the local hunts (Burton, Blankney and Grove & Rufford) under the chairmanship of Mr W F Ransom.

By late 1966, news came through that the National Hunt Committee, responsible for jump racing in Britain, had given approval for the Carholme to be used for point-to-point racing in 1967. The dates would be 8th April (Burton Hunt), 22nd April (Grove & Retford) and 10th May (Blakeney).

The news was generally greeted with much pleasure, albeit there was at least one dissenting view. The Chronicle of 25th November 1966 carried a short article, from an un-named correspondent, stating his personal opposition to the return of racing to the Carholme. The gist of his argument was that the whole idea was a *'jolly good example of a backward-looking community. Having seen the end of professional racing there was the prospect of 'threepenny rides on donkeys provided by amateur's'.* According to the correspondent, the racecourse buildings could be used as a club for young people between the ages of 17 and 21 (his one as it turned out perceptive comment) and a sports stadium. He finished off with a final disagreeable comment, questioning how many people would actually turn out to *'see a few plummy girls jumping over sticks'*!

Approval was duly given to racing by the City Council's Finance Committee, followed on 13th December 1966 by the full Council itself.

Despite the misgivings of the Chronicle's correspondent, the first point-to-point meeting was held just three days after the 1967 Lincoln Handicap, the course featuring nine fences. It was the first occasion in Lincoln's racing history where women rode competitively with the men.

The opening point to point meeting was adjudged to have been a great success, with over 4,000 hardy souls braving typically bad Carholme weather! The attendance was very encouraging, given the fact that the Grand National was being held on the same day. To compensate for this, a full commentary on the big race was broadcast over the public address system and several televisions were placed at strategic locations in the stands.

After the success of the initial meetings, the Carholme point to points quickly became established as a regular feature with both the local racing community and the general public.

Sadly 1969 saw the demolition of the historic County Stand, which had been allowed to fall into a poor state of repair. Given the fact that the stand dated from 1823, it is quite possible that in today's more conservation minded world, the building would have been listed and a valuable piece of both local and national sporting history preserved. The best surviving example of a stand from this era at Kelso Racecourse which opened in 1822. It was however designed back in 1778 by the renowned John Carr of York, also responsible for the magnificent Georgian Newark on Trent Town Hall.

In 1981 the City Council debated a proposal by Major James Barnett (retired) President of the West End Community Association, that the remaining 1879 stand be converted into a racing museum. Unfortunately, the sheer cost of refurbishing the building quickly rendered this nice idea to be impractical.

Throughout the 1970's and 1980's racing continued successfully at the Carholme but as so often in the course's history, a black cloud was looming on the horizon. The Point-to-Point Committee's licence had come up for renewal in 1991. For the past twenty-one years, the Point-to-Point Committee had operated the races under successive seven-year licences, at a fee of £2,500 per annum.

Matters came to a head when Labour City Councillor Brian Ellis asked for an assurance, that no profits raised from the point to points would go to supporting blood sports. Given that the point to points were run by the local hunts this was sure to become an issue.

Chairman of the Point-to-Point Committee Arthur Lockwood expressed to the Lincolnshire Echo, on 3rd January 1991, his concern at delays in the renewal of their licence. He also revealed that the Committee did have an alternative venue, should the Council refuse to co-operate and grant a new licence. He further confirmed that any profits from the meeting did indeed go to the Hunts. This would not however be happening for 1990, since lower gate receipts meant that a loss had been made.

Some days later, the Council's Regeneration, Leisure and Tourism Committee debated the issue at length and confirmed that, so long as the meetings were not producing funds to promote blood sports, the point to point could continue. The licence renewal was subject to three main condition's: -

(1) *The organisers would have to hand over any profits made to the Mayor's chosen charity.*
(2) *To ensure that (1) above happened, the annual accounts of the meeting would be scrutinised by the City Treasurers Department.*
(3) *No one at the meeting would be allowed to wear hunt uniform nor any publicity which could be seen to be favouring hunting.*

Whatever the rights and wrongs of blood sports, it was surely naïve in the extreme, for the Council to believe that the conditions would in any way be acceptable to a Committee run by the local hunts. In what appears to have possibly been something of a smoke screen, one of the City Councillors suggested that the race organisers were looking to move from Lincoln anyway, and the City Council were a convenient scapegoat for that move.

To no one's great surprise, the Point-to-Point Committee declined to take up the new licence on the conditions offered and no further public discussions were held on the subject.

The final Burton Hunt Meeting took place on Saturday 11th March 1991. Traditionally at the opening meeting of the year, the winner of the Gentleman's Open Race would be presented by the Mayor with the magnificent silver and gold Lincoln Cup. Unsurprisingly there was no sign of either the Mayor or the Cup.

To the South Wold Hunt came the *'honour'* of hosting the last ever race meeting on Lincoln Racecourse on 6th May 1991. Thereafter the point-to-points moved to their new home at Market Rasen.

And that finally was that as regards horse racing on the Carholme. Lincoln would not appear in any official race listings again.

Chapter Ten - One Last Throw of the Dice

The end of the point-to-points was not however the complete end of the story. In 2004 the then prospective Conservative Parliamentary candidate for Lincoln, Karl McCartney, expressed the view that he wanted to see if he could bring the grandstand and the racecourse back into use, allowing racing to take place once again on the Carholme.

In an article in The Echo from April 2009, McCartney revealed that in 2007, meetings had been held with the City Council and Doncaster based International Racecourse Management Ltd, operators of various courses including Wetherby, Thirsk and Redcar plus others in the Middle East. He advised that the discussions were only at an early stage and the City Council would want to see more detailed plans before possibly taking matters further.

He went onto further explain that *'We still have this five-year plan, but we will have to wait and see. It's difficult times with the economy but what I do know is that the investors of International Racecourse Management are not necessarily all UK based so there is a firm backing. They are now pushing to get the agreement signed and bring the investment and racing back to Lincoln'*. Plans also included the hope that the Lincoln Handicap would return to the Carholme.

Mr McCartney was clearly very confident of success, claiming 99.9% positive reaction from responses received to the idea, adding that the economic benefits to Lincoln would far outweigh any counter arguments. To allay likely concerns he stated that they were not looking to take the Common away, simply to bring it back to its *'proper use'*.

On Friday 11th June 2010 a briefing was given by Karen Rastall, who was working with Karl McCartney, unveiling plans by the Lincoln Racecourse Regeneration Company (LRRC) to bring racing back to the cities West Common. Despite the optimistic pronouncements from Mr McCartney, it is fair to say that not everyone shared his view. This was particularly the case for residents of Lincoln's nearby West End, who believed the revived course would cause major parking and traffic problems. This issue had been acknowledged by LRC, who accepted that careful planning and strategies would be needed, very much akin to the Christmas Market.

The plans (which were to be found on LRRC's website) claimed that the revived course would bring forward investment of at least £12m over the coming five to seven years. Works would include renovating the existing stand, building a new stable block, improvements to the turf, as well as new drainage for the course and adjacent areas of the Common.

It was intended that racing would take place a maximum of sixteen times a year, a large increase from the seven of years past but not excessive compared to most courses. Meetings would take place from March to October (the normal Flat Race season on Turf) with potentially up to 5000 in attendance at each meeting.

Within the proposal document there was reference to 90,000 leaflets having been delivered, seeking feedback from across Lincoln on the plans. From those who did respond, the exact number was not clear, seemingly over 97% of respondents believed the course could be of economic benefit to the City.

The intention was that plans would be developed to a point where by 2011, the public would be able to comment, and a revised final version produced. All being well, flat racing would be returning to the Carholme in around five years. However, before that, the plans would need to be considered by the City Council.

On 10th July 2010 the Lincolnite reported that an unnamed Conservative Councillor, the preference for anonymity apparently being to preserve the ability to vote on the question, believed there to be *'no general support within the Council'* for the racecourse plans, which he described as a *'complete waste of time'*. For good measure he also stated that the City of Lincoln is *'never ever going to grant them (LRRC) a lease'*.

Local opposition, led by Emile Van Der Zee of the 'Hands off our Common Campaign' had started a petition, now 450 signatures strong, opposing the plan. Backing had also come from TV botanist David Bellamy, who described the Common as *'very, very precious'* and unsuitable for any form of commercial use.

On 27th July 2010 BBC Local News announced further opposition from a panel of local interest groups called the Commons Advisory Committee. Speaking after the Committee had met, Chairman Helen Heath stated that *'Everybody round the table feels that the proposals don't really come up to scratch, that there is insufficient detail. There is no business plan, there's no financial breakdown. There are too many questions left unanswered'*.

The Council were due to consider the LRRC's plans in detail on Monday 16th August when news came through, on 13th August that LRRC had withdrawn its plans prior to the meeting. Suffice to say, the news was met with delight by opponents, who indicated that they would be bringing forward their own plans for the Common.

Commenting on the decision to withdraw Karen Rastall said, on behalf of the Company, that it was merely a deferment they were seeking. Most particularly:

'We feel the report that was tabled for Monday evening and the options that were actually outlined for the council to consider were not in keeping with the discussions we had been holding with Lincoln City Council for a considerable period of time'.

'They did not reflect the behind-the-scenes discussions that had been on the go and the information the Council had been asking for'.

In response, the City Council's Communications Manager Chris Dunbar confirmed that the meeting would take place and that, in the view of the Council, *'The report to be presented to the Executive is a fair appraisal of the proposal, taking into account both the information presented by LRRC and the comments of the Commons Advisory Panel'*

The meeting duly took place in public on Monday 16th August 2010, at which the City Council rejected the plans as being *'unsuitable'*. City Council Leader Darren Grice informed the meeting that the Council had ruled out the possibility of racing being held on the Common.

Reaction to the decision was understandably mixed. Emile Van Der Zee of the 'Hands off Our Common Campaign' was understandably delighted and confirmed that they would be concentrating on the future of the Common.

For the prospective developers, Karen Rastall expressed shock at the decision and felt very let down by the Council. The Company had requested a twelve-month lease of the course, in order to draw up a detailed business case for the return of racing. This followed on from two years of discussion with the Council, allied to there being legislation allowing racing, in principle at least, to take place on the Common.

Whatever the rights and wrongs of whether racing should have been given the chance to return, the Council's decision really did mean that racing in Lincoln was truly a thing of the past. The stand remains, with the ground floor used as a community centre, and the line-up board stands beside Carholme Roads. A number of the trophies can also still be found in Lincoln's Guild Hall.

Never perhaps the most glamorous of courses Lincoln was, courtesy of its famous Lincolnshire Handicap, the opening salvo for many years to the British Flat Racing season and enjoyed both the highs and lows of popularity.

Appendix One – Past Winners of the Lincolnshire Handicap at The Carholme

- 1849. Midia
- 1852. The Little Mare
- 1853. Caurire
- 1854. Georgey
- 1855. Saucebox
- 1856. Flageolet
- 1857. Huntingdon
- 1858. Vandermulin
- 1859. Bel Esperanza
- 1860. Vigo
- 1861. Benbow
- 1862. Suburban
- 1863. Manrico
- 1864: Benjamin
- 1865: Gaily
- 1866: Treasure Trove
- 1867: Vandervelde
- 1868: Indigestion
- 1869: Sycee
- 1870: Royal Rake
- 1871: Vulcan
- 1872: Guy Dayrell
- 1873: Vestminster
- 1874: Tomahawk
- 1875: The Gunner
- 1876: Controversy
- 1877: Footstep
- 1878: Kaleidoscope
- 1879: Touchet
- 1880: Rosy Cross
- 1881: Buchanan
- 1882: Poulet
- 1883: Knight of Burghley
- 1884: Tonans
- 1885: Bendigo
- 1886: Fulmen
- 1887: Oberon
- 1888: Veracity
- 1889: Wise Man

- 1890: The Rejected
- 1891: Lord George
- 1892: Clarence
- 1893: Wolf's Crag
- 1894: Le Nicham
- 1895: Euclid
- 1896: Clorane
- 1897: Winkfield's Pride
- 1898: Prince Barcaldine
- 1899: General Peace
- 1900: Sir Geoffrey
- 1901: Little Eva
- 1902: St Maclou
- 1903: Over Norton
- 1904: Uninsured
- 1905: Sansovino
- 1906: Ob
- 1907: Ob
- 1908: Kaffir Chief
- 1909: Duke of Sparta
- 1910: Cinderello
- 1911: Mercutio
- 1912: Long Set
- 1913: Berrilldon
- 1914: Outram
- 1915: View Law
- 1916: Clap Gate *
- 1917–18: *no race*
- 1919: Royal Bucks
- 1920: Furious
- 1921: Soranus
- 1922: Granely
- 1923: White Bud
- 1924: <u>Sir Gallahad</u>
- 1925: Tapin
- 1926: King of Clubs
- 1927: Priory Park
- 1928: Dark Warrior
- 1929: Elton
- 1930: Leonidas
- 1931: Knight Error
- 1932: Jerome Fandor

- 1933: Dorigen
- 1934: Play On
- 1935: Flamenco
- 1936: Over Coat
- 1937: Marmaduke Jinks
- 1938: Phakos
- 1939: Squadron Castle
- 1940: Quartier-Maitre
- 1941: Gloaming
- 1942: Cuerdley **
- 1943: Lady Electra **
- 1944: Backbite **
- 1945: Double Harness**
- 1946: Langton Abbot
- 1947: Jockey Treble
- 1948: Commissar
- 1949: Fair Judgement
- 1950: Dramatic
- 1951: Barnes Park
- 1952: Phariza
- 1953: Sailing Light
- 1954: Nahar
- 1955: Military Court
- 1956: Three Star
- 1957: Babur
- 1958: Babur
- 1959: Marshal Pil
- 1960: Mustavon
- 1961: Johns Court
- 1962: Hill Royal
- 1963: Monawin
- 1964: Mighty Gurkha

* The 1916 running took place at Lingfield Park in Surrey.
** The 1942 race was run as "Northern Lincoln" whilst 1943, 1944 and 1945 were run as the "Substitute Lincoln" and were all held at Pontefract in Yorkshire.

Appendix Two – Timeline

1597	Earliest reference to horse racing having taken place in Lincoln
1617	King James 1st attends the races on 3rd April 1617 on Waddington Heath
1635	Earliest recorded instance of a cup being presented for a race on the Heath
1759	Harmston Common enclosed
1770	Eclipse the 'Wonder Horse' of the 18th Century visits Waddington Heath
1770	Racing ceases on Waddington Heath
1771-2	Racing held on Welton Heath
1773	Racing begins on the Carholme
1806	Largest prize yet at 105 guineas to the winner
1826	County Stand opened
1846	Cure-All beats Vanguard in a rare meeting of two Grand National winners
1849	First Lincolnshire Handicap Run
1849	First running of the Brocklesby Stakes, still run today at Doncaster
1853	First running of the Lincoln Spring Handicap
1855	Lincolnshire won by Classic Winner Saucebox
1858	Spring Handicap and Lincolnshire Handicap merged
1871	Grand National and Lincolnshire run on same day for the only time
1874	Prize money for the Lincolnshire increased to £1000
1880	Col Brook starts his 46-year tenure on the Races Committee
1885	Lincoln hosts the prestigious National Hunt Chase
1897	A new stand, still standing today, was opened

1900	Introduction of the starting gate to British Racing
1902	Multiple Classic Winner Sceptre second in the Lincolnshire Handicap
1906	Ob becomes first French trained winner of the Lincolnshire Handicap
1907	New lease granted to Races Committee until 1920
1914	Passing of the Lincoln Corporation Act
1916	Substitute Lincolnshire Handicap run at Lingfield Park in Surrey
1930	Introduction of an on-course Tote to British racing
1934	Victory in the Lincolnshire Handicap for county trainer James Russell
1934	Film rights sold to Pathe News for the first time
1937	First year in which BBC purchases the rights to broadcast the race on the radio
1938	City Corporation forms its own Races Committee
1939	Privately owned Races Committee's lease comes to an end
1939	City Corporation announces ambitious plans for a new stand
1940	Cities plans approved by Government but put on hold due to the War
1942-5	Course closed and substitute Lincolnshire Handicap run at Pontefract
1946	Racing returns to the Carholme with crowds in excess of 100,000 people
1948	Largest ever field of 58 for Lincolnshire Handicap, a UK record for a flat race
1949	Favourite Fair Judgement wins the centenary Lincolnshire Handicap
1951	Electronic scales introduced for weighing the jockeys
1954	Race commentary broadcast over PA system for the first time
1955	Evening racing introduced for the first time
1959	BBC TV covers the Lincolnshire live on TV for the first time
1959	Races Committee announces plans for £30,000 in improvements

1962	Rumours start to circulate about potential closure
1963	Levy Board announces that support will be withdrawn for Lincoln Races
1963	Ladbrokes put up £3000 in prize money for the Lincolnshire Handicap
1964	Billy Butlin puts up £1000 sponsorship for the opening race of the Spring Meet
1964	Mighty Gurkha wins final Lincolnshire Handicap on the Carholme
1964	Last flat race to be held at the Carholme on 21st May 1964
1964	Home Secretary confirms on 21st July confirms Levy Board's decision
1965	Lincolnshire Handicap run for first time at Doncaster Racecourse
1965	Discussions begin to use Lincoln for point-to-point racing
1966	National Hunt Committee approves point to pointing at the Carholme
1967	First point to point meeting held on the Carholme
1969	Demolition of the historic County Stand takes place
1991	City Council ask Point to Point Committee to sever links with Hunting
1991	Last point to point held on the Carholme in May
2009	Lincoln Racecourse Company Ltd formed
2010	City Council formally reject re-opening of racing on the Carholme

Appendix Three – Bibliography

- 'A Long Time Gone' by Chris Pitt (the definitive guide to former racecourse in the United Kingdom)

- Biographical Encyclopaedia of British Flat Racing by Roger Mortimer, Richard Onslow and Peter Willett

- Richard Baerlin 'Joe Mercer: The Pictorial Biography'

- 'Georgian Lincoln' by Sir Francis Hill

- Paul Mathieu 'The Druids Lodge Confederacy'

- Edward Hide 'Nothing to Hide'

- Lincolnshire Echo (Various)

- Lincolnshire Chronicle (Various)

- Ruffs Guide to the Turf

- The Lincolnite